Jill Tweedie has been writing a weekly column in the *Guardian* for ten years and has received both Granada Television and IPC awards for Best Woman Journalist of the Year. For two years she presented Thames Television's *Good Afternoon* and she broadcasts regularly on both radio and television.

Jill Tweedie

In the Name of Love

A PALADIN BOOK

GRANADA
London Toronto Sydney New York

Published by Granada Publishing Limited in 1980

ISBN 0 586 08348 0

First published in Great Britain by
Jonathan Cape Ltd 1979
Copyright © Jill Tweedie 1979

Granada Publishing Limited
Frogmore, St Albans, Herts AL2 2NF
and
3 Upper James Street, London W1R 4BP
866 United Nations Plaza, New York, NY 10017, USA
117 York Street, Sydney, NSW 2000, Australia
100 Skyway Avenue, Rexdale, Ontario, M9W 3A6, Canada
PO Box 84165, Greenside, 2034 Johannesburg, South Africa
61 Beach Road, Auckland, New Zealand

Set, printed and bound in Great Britain by
Cox & Wyman Ltd, Reading
Set in Intertype Baskerville

Granada ®
Granada Publishing ®

*To all those men with whom this book
would never have been written*

'But these are all lies: men have died from time to time, and worms have eaten them, but not for love.'

Rosalind, in *As You Like It*,
Act IV, Scene 1

'Please – a little less love, and a little more common decency.'

Kurt Vonnegut, in *Slapstick
or Lonesome No More!*

Contents

Acknowledgments

I should like to thank Dory Previn and Dorothy Dinnerstein for talking to me and allowing me to quote from their books, respectively *Midnight Baby* and *The Rocking of the Cradle and the Ruling of the World*. I am also indebted to Gitta Sereny for letting me reproduce some parts of her conversation with Frau Stangl from *Into That Darkness*; to Bantam Books, New York, for permission to quote from Susan Atkins's *Child of Satan, Child of God* and to Doubleday and Co., Inc., New York, for Marge Piercy's poem 'Women's Laughter', from her book *To Be of Use*.

The verse 'The mind has a thousand eyes' (p. 11) is by F. W. Bourdillon and appears in *Poems of Today*, Sidgwick and Jackson, 1924. The song 'I'll String Along with You' (p. 159), © 1934 by Warner Bros Inc., is quoted by permission of B. Feldman and Co. Ltd, and 'Bachelor Gay' (p. 192), © 1917 by Francis Day and Hunter Ltd, by permission of EMI Music Publishing Ltd, both of 138–40 Charing Cross Road, London WC2H OLD.

My warmest thanks to André Schiffrin of Pantheon who launched the enterprise with tea at Fortnum and Mason's, to Liz Calder for her unfailing support and to my editor, Deborah Shepherd, for her sharp eyes.

And finally, my gratitude to The Ship at Deal and those who sail in her, for providing a refuge of friendship whenever love became too much.

A NOTE

Throughout this book I often use the word 'marriage' as a shorthand term for any relationship of some duration between two people, heterosexual or homosexual, with or without benefit of clergy or clerk, that involves physical intercourse and has some central emotional or social importance to the partners concerned.

Preface

Love, it seems, is as much a part of the unique equipment of homo sapiens as language or laughter and far more celebrated. If all the words that have been written about it since mankind first put stick to clay were laid end to end, they would rocket past Venus and vanish into deep space. Histories of love, philosophies of love, psychologies of love, guidebooks to love, love letters, love hymns, love stories, love poems, love songs have covered tablets and papyrus, parchment and paper and walls, filled theatres across time and lands from Epidaurus to Radio City, and been declaimed by gods and goddesses of love from Sappho to Warren Beatty. Love has been, is now and ever shall be our scourge and balm, our wound and salve, source of our finest and most bestial actions, the emotion that passeth all understanding. It is a heavenly body out of our orbit, beyond man-made laws, ethics or control, a magical splendour that descends upon us like the gift of tongues and possesses us whether we will or no. Love transforms us into something strange and rare, it ignites our lives and, dying, takes all meaning away.

> The mind has a thousand eyes
> And the heart but one
> Yet the light of a whole life dies
> When love is done.

We die of love and die without it, our hearts beat for it and break for it. Love built the Taj Mahal, wrote the Song of Solomon and cooks a billion meals every day, across the world. Love is the only thing that matters at all, after all.

Or so they say. And in my opinion what they say, give or take an epigram or two, is rubbish. Take off the rose-coloured glasses and what does a close examination of the facts reveal to the naked eye? That love, true love, is the rarest of all the emotions and one that has been conspicuous only by its absence ever since mankind dropped from the trees. If we condense the earth's history into one calendar year, homo sapiens appeared in the late evening of 31 December and love, his much-vaunted race-long companion, is still merely a glimmer on the midnight horizon of the coming New Year. Love, in other words, inhabits the future, a kind of reverse star whose light reaches us before it is born instead of after it has died. Certainly, intimations of love's coming have touched an individual here and there through time and its prophets have started new religions, composed great symphonies, made beautiful sculpture and painted exquisite canvases. But for the wide river of humanity, the ordinary mass of men and women who have peopled our planet and reproduced our race, love was not necessary, not possible and not there.

Why, then, the stories, the poems and the songs, the jubilations and the suicides? How can you argue that love does not exist when human beings deliberately end their own existence for love? Surely nothing is as indisputable as that love and mankind go hand in hand. I love, therefore I am. But is it love they feel? I think not. The word is a vast umbrella that covers a multitude of virtues and sins and because we are perfectly familiar with all of love's precursors and understudies, we imagine that we have pinned down love itself when we have merely trapped its shadow. Co-operation, for instance, midwife to that most ancient of drives, survival. You scratch my back and I'll scratch yours. Sex, a powerhouse so overwhelming in its assault upon us that, trying to domesticate it, we have given it the prettier name of love. We know about affection and friendship. We feel liking, duty, deference, greed, lust, ambition, attraction, protectiveness, ingratiation and the desire to conform. We are gripped by infatuation, obsession, adoration, vanity, addiction, jealousy, fear and the dread of being alone. Very deeply we know about need. I need you. He needs me. Needs must.

But love is somewhere else and all those other drives and needs and feelings are like the gases that swirl about in space, inwardly spiralling through the centuries to centre at last on a small hard core, gases that are only hot air in themselves but essential for the eventual formation of a new world, a world of real love. We may arrive at it one day, given time, but we are not there yet.

ONE

The Experience

'Some day my prince will come . . .'

I have no particular qualifications to write about love but then, who has? There are no courses of higher learning offered in the subject except at the University of Life, as they say, and there I have put in a fair amount of work. So I offer my own thoughts, experiences and researches into love in the only spirit possible to such an enterprise – a combination of absolute humility and utter arrogance that will cause the reader either to deride my wrong-headedness or, with luck, to recognize some of the same lessons.

I am a white, Anglo-Saxon, heterosexual, happily married, middle-income female whose experience of what is called love spans forty years of the mid-twentieth century in one of the most fortunate parts of the globe. I mention this because I am profoundly aware of the limits these facts give to my vision; also because, in spite of such advantages, my experience of love has hardly been uplifting and yet, because of them too, I have at least been vouchsafed a glimpse of what love might be, some day.

I took my first steps in what I was told was love when the idea of high romance and living happily ever after still held sway. They said that whatever poisoned apple I might bite would surely be dislodged by a Prince's kiss and I would then rise from all the murderous banalities of living and, enfolded in a strong man's arms, gallop away on a white charger to the better land called love. The way it turned out, this dream of love did not do much to irradiate my life. The ride was nice enough but 'twas better to travel than to arrive and – oh, shame – there was more than one Prince. Of two previous marriages and a variety of other lovings, very little remains and that mostly ugly. However sweet love's initial presence, when it goes it leaves horrid scars. Unlike friendship and other forms of love, the tide of male/female sex love does not ebb imperceptibly, leaving the stones it reveals gleaming and covetable. No. It only shows that what was taken to be precious is simply a bare, dull pebble like any other.

Loving, lovers fill each other's lives, Siamese twins joined at the heart, bees that suck honey from each other's blossoms. When love ebbs, nothing remains. Ex-lovers rarely meet again or write or offer each other even those small kindnesses and comforts that strangers would not withhold. Birthdays, high days and holidays pass unmarked where once they were entered in New Year diaries and planned for months ahead. Photographs of the beloved are discarded or curl up, yellowing, in some dusty drawer. What was once the world becomes a no-man's-land, fenced with barbed wire, where trespassers are prosecuted and even the civilities given a passing acquaintance are forbidden. What was most intimate – private thoughts, dreams, nightmares and childhood panics soothed in warm arms – are now merely coinage for a pub joke, a hostess flippancy, worth a line or two in the local paper or the old school magazine. Divorced. Separated. Split.

For the first man I thought I loved, and therefore married, I bear, at most, a distant anger for injuries received. For the second I carefully suppress the good times, burying them with the bad. All those hours, weeks, months, years passed in the same bed have vanished leaving only the traces of an old wound, an ache where a growth was removed.

Was either a part of love, ever? Of a kind. The best we could manage at the time, a deformed seedling planted in infertile ground. The three of us, each of them and me, carried loads on our backs when we met, all the clobber of past generations. This I must do, that you must be, this is good, that is bad, you must, I must, we must. By the time we met we were already proficient puppeteers, hands stuck up our stage dolls, our real selves well concealed behind the striped canvas. You Punch, me Judy. Me Jane, you Tarzan.

I had a conventional 1940s and 1950s childhood, cut to the pattern of time. I adored and admired my father and my father did not adore or admire me. My mother was there like the curtains and the carpets were there, taken for loving granted in early childhood and then ruthlessly discarded, the living symbol of everything my world did not regard and that I, therefore, did not wish to become. Rejecting her caused a very slight wreckage inside, nothing you'd notice, though transfusions would later be necessary. Powerful unloving father, powerless loving mother. Cliché.

So I did what I could to make my way and married an older man. Love and marriage go together like a horse and carriage. This act imposed certain conditions. First of all, you cannot grow up if you marry a father figure because this is no part of the contract, and besides, growing up is a disagreeable occupation. Then, of course, a continuing virginity of mind, if not of body, is essential because Daddy's girl has never known other men and any evidence of sexual curiosity or, worse, a touch of ribaldry might cause him to withdraw his protection. Indeed, a daughter must not know much of anything at all because Daddy must teach and daughter learn, for ever. Competence, independence, self-sufficiency, talent in anything but the most girlish endeavours, toughness of any kind, is against the rules. Lightheartedness, giggling, little tantrums and a soupçon of mischief are permitted because Daddy is a Daddy, after all, and likes to be amused after a long day or even smack a naughty bum, in his wisdom. My first marriage was a romper room and each day I laid plans to negotiate the next, with my thumb stuck endearingly in my mouth.

To begin with, we both enjoyed the game we didn't know we were playing. He was a proper husband in the eyes of the outside world, protective and admonitory, and I was a proper wife, that is to say, a child; charming and irresponsible. But quite soon these playful rituals began to harden into concrete, so that we could no longer move, even if we wished, as long as we were together. For a few years I was satisfied enough, the drama of my life absorbed me, it was a stage and I was the star. First a house to play with and later, in case the audience began to cough and fidget, a pregnancy to hold them riveted. Later, like Alice in Wonderland, I came across the cake labelled 'eat me' and whenever my husband was away at work, I ate and I grew. My legs stuck out of the windows, my arms snaked round the doors, my head above an endless neck loomed through the chimney and my heartbeat rocked the room. Each day, just before 5 p.m., I nibbled the other side of Alice's cake and, in the nick of time, shrank to being a little woman again. Hullo, darling, how was your day? Me? Oh, nothing happened. Terrified, I knew that one day I wouldn't make it down again and my husband, returning from work, would fall back in horror at the monster who had taken over his home and push me out into the big wide world.

Writing this now perhaps suggests that I was aware of a pretence and set up my false self knowingly, for reward. Not so. The boundaries given me in girlhood were strictly defined, allowing only minimum growth and that mainly physical. To sprout the titivating secondary sexual characteristics was expected, but woe betide the *enfant terrible* who tried to burst that tight cocoon and emerge as a full-grown adult in mind as well as body. The penalty was ill-defined but all-pervasive, like those sci-fi novels of a post-nuclear generation bred to fear the radioactive world above their subterranean tunnels that threatens isolation, mutilation and death. The reward for my self-restraint (in the most literal sense) was a negative one – be good and tractable and you will be looked after – but it was none the less powerful for that. So my real self, or hints of it, was as frightening to me as I feared it would be to my husband, a dark shadow given to emerging at less and less acceptable times. I was Mr Rochester secure in his mansion but I was also his mad wife in the attic. I had to conceal her existence to preserve my way of life but all the time she was setting matches to the bedding, starting a flame at the hem of the curtains, hoping to burn the mansion down.

Things became more and more schizoid. The demure façade of a prim girl hid a raucous fishwife who folded her massive arms against her chest and cursed. She horrified me, so much so – threatening, as she did, my exile from society – that in spite of increasing marital quarrels and even spurts of pure hatred, never once did I let that fishwife out to hurl the oaths she could have hurled or yelled the truths she knew. How could I, without revealing what I really was, to him and to myself?

The inner split opened wider. When my husband said he loved me, I knew he meant he loved the doll I had created and I accepted his love smugly enough, on her behalf. She was worth it. She wore the right clothes, she said the right things, the span of her waist would bring tears to your eyes and the tiny staccato of her heels across a floor would melt the sternest heart. She turned her head upon its graceful stem just so and her camellia hands, laced on her lap, could make a stone bleed. She smiled just enough to give a man the wildest expectations and frowned just enough to make him feel safe. This doll is a good doll. This doll is a marriageable doll. This doll is a real doll.

I knew, of course, that my doll self was only a front but it was the one I had deliberately created in response to popular demand. My real self knew all the things the doll did not wish to know. She was human and therefore hopelessly un-feminine, she had no pretty ways. Her voice was harsh, pumped from the guts instead of issuing sweetly from the throat, and every now and then she howled and the doll was forced to look at her face, bare as a picked bone. No wonder the poor dolly gathered up her ruffled skirts and ran shriek-ing down corridors to find reassurance in a man's eyes. See my soft red lips, my white skin, feel how smooth the shaven legs, smell the scented underarms, tell me you love me, dolly me.

There were, of course, other ways to accommodate the spectre within and other ways became more necessary as the spectre grew stronger and rattled the bars of the cage. My husband was a man of uncertain temper. I was quite aware of this before we married. He came from a country ravaged by war, his home had been destroyed, his brother killed, his family made refugees and he, corralled off the streets of his town, had spent two years starving in the polar wastes of a Russian prison camp. Understandably, he was outside the conventional pale. I was afraid of him.

The fear was seductive. The dolly shook with it at times, was martyred by it. Hit, punched, she fell to the floor and lay, a poor pale victim, her lashes fanned against an appealingly white cheek stained, briefly, dull red. Later, kindly, she accepted the remorse of her attacker, grovelling before her. Yes, I forgive you, she said. And well she might forgive, because down in the dungeon beneath, her other self was quiet for the time being, gorged to quiescence on the thick hot adrenalin provided by the man. A small price to pay.

I do not know how many people stand at the altar repeating the marriage vows and knowing, however unclearly, that what they say is false and what they do calamitous. My doll stood stiffly in her stiff dress, the groom beside her, and there was not a hope for them. Upbringing had set us against each other from the start and each was busily preparing to hammer the other into an appropriate frame. After the service well-wishers launched our raft with champagne; lashed together, not far out, we sank.

Next time, I chose more carefully. The doll, anyway, was aware that her days were numbered. Winning ways must be adjusted if they are to go on being useful and a good actress acknowledges that she has aged out of *ingénue* roles before the casting director says don't call us. Besides, I was no longer enamoured of my puppet and did not want to extend her life much further. She had become more obstacle than defence, the way a wall, originally built to keep enemies out, can come to be a prison keeping you in.

So I let my real self out on probation, to be called in only now and then for discipline. And now I needed a male with all the right worldly appurtenances, whom I could use as a hermit crab uses a shell, to reach full growth without exposing vulnerable flesh. Using him, I could flex my own muscles in safety until they were strong enough to risk exposure.

So I fell in love with my second husband. This time, the emotion was much more powerful because I knew he had seen something of my real self before he took me on. I thought him beautiful, a golden man, flamboyant and seductively hollow, like a rocket into which I could squeeze myself and guide the flight, using his engines. He was so large he filled a room, his laugh set it shaking, his shining head topped everyone, he drew all eyes. In the turmoil of his wake I found breathing space, I could advance or retreat as I chose. He had another desirable asset and that was his lack of self-restraint. He never talked if he could shout, he never saved if he could spend, he was full of tall stories and the drinks were always on him. All of which combined to make him a natural force and natural forces can be harnessed for other ends. By his noisy, infuriating, unpredictable, ebullient and blustering existence he made me look, in comparison, a good, calm, reasonable and deeply feminine woman and thus I was able over the years with him, to allow my real self out for airings in the sure knowledge that though I might not be as adorable as the doll, I was bound to appear more acceptable than I actually was.

There were drawbacks, of course. Originally, the space within our relationship was almost entirely taken up with the volume of his ego and I made do in a little left-over corner. He breathed deeply, his lungs fully expanded, and I breathed lightly, in short thin gasps, and there was air enough for both of us. But then things changed. I learned a trade, began to work, worked hard and earned money. Hey, he said, getting a little stuffy in here, isn't it? Sorry, darling, I said. I breathed more deeply and new ideas rushed in. The voices of American women reached me, ideas on women's rights that linked me to the clamour of the outside world. For the first time I saw myself face to face, recognized myself, realized that I was not my own creation, uniquely formed in special circumstances, but much of a muchness with other women, a fairly standard female product made by a conveyor-belt society. Inner battles, to be fought for myself alone, became outer battles, to be fought alongside the whole female sex. Release, euphoria. Look, said my husband, I haven't enough room. Neither have I, I said. I would not placate, I would not apologize, I would not give ground any more because I was connected now to a larger army that waged a bigger war, and rescue was at hand. The slaves had revolted and even the most abject gained strength for their individual skirmishes from the growing awareness that they were not personally slavish but merely enslaved. My poor man had his problems, too, but I felt no pity, then. The walls of our relationship were closing in, we fought each other as the oxygen gave out and finally I made it into the cold, invigorating fresh air. The dolly died of double pneumonia but I was still alive.

That is a brief sketch of two marriages, founded on something we all called love because we lived in the romantic West and what other reason is allowed for marriage, if not love? On the surface, of course, the upheavals were not so apparent, being thought of as private quarrels, and I have anyway condensed them greatly – they were actually spread over seven years each, the seven years they say it takes a human to replace every cell of body skin. In the lulls between there were good times, when we laughed together and shared quite a deal of tenderness and celebrated the birth of children, and just ordinary times when we went about the business of marriage, the paying of bills, the buying of goods, the cooking and the cleaning and the entertainment of friends, as every couple does. I make very little of them because the world made so much, crowding round the happy wife, the successful husband, and abruptly turning away, turning a blind and embarrassed eye to the sobbing wife and the angry, frustrated husband. Besides, the violence was endemic and perhaps because of that, ignored as much as possible. Each of us thought we were building new houses, especially designed for us, but we didn't know about the quicksand beneath or the death-watch beetles munching the timbers. An all-pervading dishonesty hung over our enterprise. I was not what I pretended and neither were they. I sold my soul for a mess of sacrificial femininity, sugar and spice and all things nice. They built a prison with their own masculinity, so constricting it made them red in the face, choleric. And the impulsion to act out our roles, the sheer effort it took, left little time or energy to investigate small sounds of protest within. What reward, anyway, would there be for such investigation? In fact, only penalties would be paid. Loss of social approval, isolation from friends and family, accusations of bizarre behaviour and, for the woman, selfishness, that sin forbidden to any female unless she be extraordinarily rich, beautiful or old. To let the human being show behind the mask of gender was to risk even madness. They might come and take us away to the funny farm, make arrangements for derangement.

Much safer to be what they wanted, what was considered respectable. Much better to lean heavily upon each other for support and set up a quarrel, some drama, whenever the inner voices grew querulous and needed to be drowned. *Men,* said my mother, wiping my tears away. *Women,* said my father, soothing a husband. They sounded calm and quite pleased. Well, it was all very natural, wasn't it?

Long before all this, in my very first close encounter with the opposite sex, the pattern was laid down. I was ten at the time and jaunted daily back and forth to school on a bus. Every morning a boy was also waiting at the stop, he with his mates and I with mine. I liked the way he looked, I laughed a little louder when he was about. One afternoon, on the way home, it happened. I was sitting right at the front of the bus and he was two rows behind. There came a rustle, sounds of suppressed mirth, a hand stuck itself over my shoulder and thrust a small piece of paper at me. I unfolded it. There upon the graph-lined page were fat letters in pencil. 'Dear Girl,' said the letters, 'I love you.'

I read the message and stared out of the window and watched the grass that lined the road grow as green as emeralds, as if a light had been lit under every leaf. An ache started at my chest and spread through every vein until I was heavy, drugged with glucose, banjaxed by that most potent of love-surrogates – thick undiluted narcissism. A boy, a stranger, a member of the male sex, encased in his own unknown life, lying on his unknown bed, had thought of me and, by doing so, given me surreality. Until that moment 'I' was who I thought I was. From then on for a very long time, 'I' was whoever a man thought I was. That pencilled note signalled the end of an autonomy I was not to experience again for many years. As I turned towards that boy, tilting my chin, narrowing my eyes, pulling down my underlip to show my pearly teeth, giving him my first consciously manufactured, all synthetic skin-deep smile, I entered into my flawed inheritance.

Looking back on all this and other episodes of lust and affection, encounters that lasted a week or a year, the picture seems at first glance chaotic and a gloomy sort of chaos at that. Love and failure. By the standards of my time, success in love is measured in bronze and gold and diamonds, anniversaries of the day when love was firstly publicly seen to be there, at the altar. Thus I am found wanting, like any other whose marriage and relationships have ended in separation, and to be found wanting is meant to induce a sense of failure because those who do not conform must be rendered impotent.

In fact, people of my generation, like all the generations before, have had little chance of success in love of any kind. Many of those who offer the longevity of their marriage as proof of enduring love are often only revealing their own endurance in the face of ravaging compromises and a resulting anaesthesia that has left them half-way dead. In the name of that love they have jettisoned every grace considered admirable in any other part or act of life: honesty, dignity, self-respect, courtesy, kindness, integrity, steadfastness of principle. They have said those things to each other that are unsayable and done those things that are undoable and there is no health in them. They have not been true to themselves and therefore they are false to everyone else, including their children. The man has become and been allowed to become an autocrat, a tin-pot dictator in love's police state. The woman has lowered herself upon the floor to lick his jackboots. Or, sometimes, vice versa. What would never have been permitted strangers is given a free licence under love – abuse, insults, petty denigration, physical attack, intrusions on personal privacy, destruction of personal beliefs, destruction of any other friendships, destruction of sex itself. In order to enter the kingdom of love they have shrunk themselves to the space of less than one and, atrophied in every part, they claim love's crown. Two individuals who could have reached some stature have settled for being pygmies whose life's work, now, is the similar distortion of their offspring.

If love takes any other form than this tight, monogamous, heterosexual, lifelong reproductive unit, blessed by the law, the State, the priests and sanctified by gods, it is dismissed as an aberration, hounded as a perversion, insulted as a failure and refused the label 'love'. The incredible shrinking couple is presented to the world as the central aim and reward of life, a holy grail for which it is never too early to begin searching. Worst of all, we are given to believe that these dwarfish twosomes form the rock upon which all the rest of life is built, from the mental health of children to whole political systems and to remain outside it is to opt out of a cosmic responsibility and threaten the very roots of the human community. Love is all, they say. Love makes the world go round, they say. And you know it's true love, they say, when two people remain together from youth to death.

But you don't and it doesn't and you can't. The truth is that we have not yet created upon this earth the conditions in which true love can exist. Most of us are quite aware that most of mankind's other developments, emotional or technological, have been dependent upon certain prerequisites. Fire had to be discovered before we could develop a taste for cooked food and a pot to cook it in. Mass literacy was only possible after the invention of printing and printing itself depended on the much earlier Chinese discovery of papermaking. The geodesic dome was an absolute impossibility before the computer age. The emotions are based on something of the same rules. Men's lives were not overshadowed by the certainty of death (and this is still so in some primitive tribes) until life itself was safer and death could be seen inevitably to arrive without sudden injury or accident. Unlike his fellow Greeks, Xenophanes was a monotheist, largely because he guessed that the physical characteristics of the earth changed with time and belief in one universal god is dependent upon belief in universal rules. And man can only be said to have become truly self-conscious after Freud's delineation of the unconscious. Just so has love its necessary prerequisites, its birth-time in history, its most favourable climatic conditions.

So for all that we lay claim to an eternal heritage of love, man's bosom companion since the dawn of time, we have got it wrong. We have called other emotions love and they do not smell as sweet. Love itself has been very nearly impossible for most of us most of our history and is only just becoming possible today. I failed in love, like many others, because given the tools I had to hand the work could not be done. More hopelessly still, the very blueprint was flawed, a rough sketch of the eventual edifice without a single practical instruction, without a brick or a nail, without a vital part or principle. Dreams are not enough.

TWO

The Source

'I want a girl, just like the girl that
married dear old Dad.'

Mother love has always been seen as the original and illus-
trious blueprint for adult heterosexual love, a sure and abid-
ing source and model. We do not see it as conditional upon
anything, mother love simply *is,* an emotion sprung as
cleanly and asexually from the womb as Athene sprang from
her father's temple. We watch mother animals care for and
protect their young, we count ourselves infinitely superior to
them, we add the sacramental blessing of our gods and lo, we
come up with the nearest thing to perfection on earth, the
love of the mother for her child.

In bleak reality, however, mother love is dependent upon
exactly the same preconditions as any other love and is composed of many of the same ingredients. If none or only some
of these exist, then mother love does not, or only partially
exists. The all-powerful maternal instinct which is presumed
to be the root, branch and stem of human kind is no more
able to flourish without the proper environment than is adult
sexual love and so when the root of the first is stunted, the
second does not flower.

Non-human mothers protect and care for their young
only within certain fairly rigid limits. The rules are well-
defined and inexorable and survival of the fittest is the legis-
lator. The mother's job is to devote her energies to raising
those infants healthy enough to make it to adulthood, a stern
task that sometimes means starving or killing the runts or
even the infanticide of a whole litter for her own self-
preservaion, so that the show may go on. Her maternity is
directed by the bleakest instinctual practicalities and if she
must kill her infants she does so not out of some urge to protect them but because, eating them as she will then do, she

27

provides herself with the necessary recycled energy to breed again. In general, the simpler the creature, the more minimal but predictable is its caring for its young. The more complex animals, having yielded rigid instinctual behaviour for learning, are less predictable, though capable of a more thorough and long-lasting mothering. Such gregarious and instinctual species as rooks or starlings do not, if isolated from their kind, fail to carry out maternal tasks when later mated; but many animals, denied certain preconditions, lose or never learn maternal behaviour and become anything from indifferent to downright brutal towards their offspring. A female monkey, reared alone, is so drastically deprived that she becomes either a neglectful or 'battering' mother or refuses to mate at all.

And the history of human motherhood has its roots in similar preconditions and reactions. Whether we track the path of mother love in one twentieth-century woman or start way back in the dim world of the primeval mother of humanity, mulier sapiens, roaming the plains on her hind legs, clutching her infant to her with newly adapted arms, something bleaker and more imperative than love unites them. Sorting through the academic research that plunges into the past and emerges with few facts and massive assumptions, it is safe enough to say that motherhood in animals and in generations of mankind was more a question of selection for survival than of any more altruistic emotion. Indeed, sociobiologists define even altruism as a survival mechanism and ascribe the maternal instinct to the mother's need to nurture the half-share of her own genes invested in her infant.

We tend to think of human reproduction as a quality-over-quantity process, a few infants receiving such excellent individual attention that they survive to adulthood, rather than the carrying on of the species by sheer numbers, like fish. In fact, most of the available data point towards the fish principle. Until very late in our human day, women gave birth as often as they were physically equipped to do (reckoned at an average of sixteen times by experts) and it was these numbers rather than quality of care that ensured new generations.

It is likely that the early female presented herself for mating and, once impregnated, retired to the company of other females because marauding males were a constant threat to her progeny, like the lion today who will kill the cubs that are not his own. Yet this protection is no proof of maternal love. Offspring were perceived as a physical part of the mother and she reacted accordingly, in self (or gene) defence. And what little evidence there is of early matriarchies proves nothing of mothers doting on individual children. The academics who conjure up this distant era agree, on the evidence available, that the mother's sole concern was with the most vulnerable, the nursing infant, and her concern abruptly ended at the birth of a new brother or sister. The bond between mother and child lasted only as long as milk in the breast was reserved for the baby. When another newborn arrived, mewling for the nipple, the older infant was necessarily displaced and, to a great extent, forgotten. Matriarchies in history, legend and myth were marked by a ritual sacrifice that symbolized the essence of maternity. A young man, beautiful and beloved, was selected from the community, crowned King and offered to the Goddess, via any suitable lady or high priestess or Queen deemed to represent that Goddess in human form. The two wed or lived together and were indulged by the community for one year. At the end of that time, the young King was killed and replaced by another beautiful youth. Nothing more aptly symbolized the mother's natural priorities. The newborn is King in Paradise until Paradise is lost and he ejected, to make room for the next newborn. This matriarchal ritual springs straight from natural events, sans malice aforethought, untrammelled by the neocortex, a simple mirror of the facts of primitive motherhood that chills us with its ruthless inevitability and its resignation to biological destiny.

No beginning, then, in the matriarchies, of the indissoluble ties of mother to child taken so for granted in our society. No beginning of the empathy that breeds an individual love, the ability to distinguish one from another and feel more or less, accordingly. The Greeks, in whom we choose to see many echoes of our own times, seem hung about with the matriarchal doom of inevitability rather than the later, patriarchal and man-made fate. In a sense, they were attempting to bridge a growing emotional gap between the old matriarchal 'nature' and the newer patriarchal order. Emerging guilts were represented by the Furies who, for instance, bedevilled Orestes for killing his mother and Oedipus for his patricide and incest, yet the guilt itself was still essentially 'mother-innocent' and the deeds judged independently of motive. Oedipus did not intend to kill his father or sleep with his mother, his guilt was not yet introjected, it remained outside him, in the raging Erinyes, but it got him in the end. He was a scapegoat for thoughts and emotions as yet only faintly glimpsed by his fellow human beings.

And what are we to think of the legend of Medea? Euripides cast her as a witch but hinted, nevertheless, that she might merely be a strange, clever and powerful human female. When Jason fled with her and her small brother Absyrtus, Medea, in order to put her father off the chase, cut her brother into little pieces and scattered them in the wake of the boat. Later comes the part we all know – Medea kills her own children when Jason deserts her to take another wife. Could this act deserve to be made into legend, in a civilization that frequently exposed its newborn children? Or was it so heinous not because mother love failed but because Medea killed in order to deprive Jason of his lineage? A first, fierce feminist, you could call Queen Medea, but certainly no great shakes as a mother.

Later, a wandering prophet from the first truly patriarchal culture of Judaea, some two thousand years ago in the sandstone mountains of Israel, gave a pronouncement about children that was to remain more or less isolated in its understanding of their need for special tenderness right up to our own times. He said Aramaic words to the effect that whoever harmed a child, it were better he had a millstone tied about his neck and was thrown into the sea. It seems no one was listening. At any rate, the idea that children needed particular care, not to mention a particular mother love, did not emerge for a very long time to come. It is hard, looking back from our child-centred culture, where it is taken for granted (though by no means always realistically) that children are different from adults and mothers automatically love and sacrifice for them, to realize that most of history is a record of a vast indifference, if not actual cruelty, towards our own and other people's offspring.

Today, in the West, medical advances have made a child's death so rare that its happening can scar parents for life. But for some thousands of years (and still, at present, in some parts of the world) the death of children was a commonplace and when most mothers were likely to outlive all but, say, three of their sixteen infants, a certain dispassion or, at the very least, resignation would have been essential for mental health. In some ways this puts the cart before the horse, because there seems little doubt that it was in large part the mother's neglect of her infant that caused its death in the first place. Obviously, we cannot blame her for an ignorance of the causes of disease or for her own poverty which gave her child a wretched diet. Indeed, we cannot blame her at all for lacking modern attitudes and emotions that were no possible part of her repertoire. We see the same neglect and indifference among those women who were not impoverished; who had, in fact, fairly or very comfortable lives. Those who could afford it sent their infants off to wet-nurses in the country, a practice that was common throughout the Middle Ages and continued into the ninteenth century. The mere separation of infant from mother is not, perhaps, the sole criterion for judging an absence of maternal love – the upper classes in England have long made a practice of sending their sons to boarding schools at the most tender ages and though some mothers may have done so happily, many were hurt and upset by a custom that they followed because they thought it 'the right thing to do', a sacrifice demanded of them in order to give their sons a good education and the proper contacts for future success.

But the wet-nurse syndrome cannot be put in this category for the simple reason that the death rate of the farmed-out infants reached colossal proportions at times and was enormously higher than for children nursed at home by their mothers. In eighteenth-century Rouen, for example, legitimate infants cared for by their mothers had a mortality rate of 19 per cent compared to the 38 per cent of babies sent to rural foster-mothers. Of the 2,400 nurslings sent from Paris to the neighbourhood of Nogent-le-Rotrou from 1858 to 1859, 35 per cent died within the first two years of life compared with 22 per cent of country infants kept at home. It is clear, then, that even the dimmest of parents must have been aware that sending their children away meant an appreciable increase in the chances that they would never be seen alive again. Besides, many mothers did not even visit their infants to find out for themselves the conditions in which they were kept. An odd letter or two and a standard form filled out by the wet-nurse was often all the reassurance they asked for and if the infant died, well then, it died. An Act of God, of course, and not an act of Mother. The wet-nurses themselves were usually abjectly poor agricultural labourers, landless peasants or unwed mothers who actually gave birth in order to produce the milk that would earn them a living. They lived in cold and horribly overcrowded hovels thick with grime, and it is hardly surprising that their nurslings died like flies. The women were at least as indifferent to those wretched infants as their own parents and had their charges managed to endure the physical squalor of the surroundings they were unlikely to survive the continual neglect and lack of affection. Peasant women would swaddle the baby and pin the stiff little bundle to a board which they hung on a nail while they went off to work in the fields. The child, unnaturally immobile, soaked in its own excrement and unfed for hours at a time, would howl until strength left it, its pathetic cries quite probably mingling with those of the woman's own baby hanging beside it. If the baby was a foundling, farmed out by town agencies to the country, it had even less chance of survival – in Rouen, in the same year that 38 per cent of legitimate wet-nursed children died, foundlings had a mortality rate of 90 per cent.

To our modern and perhaps hypocritical eyes, these women – mothers and mercenaries – appear to be monsters, inexplicably lacking in what we consider one of womankind's most instinctual virtues, mother love. But the lack must be seen in its far wider context – love between adults was hardly extant and the day-to-day struggle for survival overrode all other things. If the love between mother and child is the root of later, adult love – and most of us agree that this is so – then that root had not yet taken and so the flower was still invisible.

Our own society is often called 'child-centred', an implicit acknowledgment of a previously different state of affairs. Children have acquired a status and a love quite new in history and it is perhaps not a coincidence that this change came about as economic circumstances began to force adults out of their close tribal groups and drive them into the city market-places, into isolation and into the self-definition necessary to combat that isolation. Historians are fond of pointing out that children in the past were considered merely miniature adults, deficient in height as in knowledge, dwarf savages to be tamed and civilized, but they do not emphasize enough that this was also the way adults thought of other adults who differed from them in wealth, class, race, colour or creed. In traditional communities, the individual had his pigeon-hole ordained from birth, he was born a slave or a serf, a yeoman or a lord and only physical growth was necessary for him to claim his heritage. Introspection, the reaction to separation from the group that reveals underlying similarities between all human beings, was rare. Economic or class change, the flexibility of the future, was in general unknown and so the concept of personality development was hardly likely to be understood. The idea of the unfolding of a child, helped and guided by an individual mother's love and care, could gain little foothold in such a rigid world. Children just growed, like Topsy, and love was not considered any vital ingredient in this growth.

Today, this change is encapsulated in each individual life; most of us now take for granted that we have a 'right' to self-fulfilment and see our lives, however hazily, as some sort of unfolding or progression, whether to intellectual maturity or simply to the heights of pleasurable experience: cars, houses, washing machines. The struggle for survival is no longer as tough and so most of us can afford to pause and devote our time to caring for our children. But still some echoes of the old ways linger and we revert with frightening ease to an ancient indifference or a view of children as obstacles to survival, to be battered or neglected until we are, one way or another, rid of them. If circumstances are difficult or impossible the human mother, just like the mothers of all other species, may follow the evolutionary imperative and cut her losses.

My own experiences of motherhood cannot be unique. When the first pains of the first labour struck at my back I felt, oddly, an imminent sense of doom. Once, long ago, I had stood on a balcony overlooking the stretch of water that separates Asia from Europe and felt an eerie wind that did not come and go but came and came, stronger and stronger, until the trees bent and my hands clenched on the wrought iron and the adults said, sharply, come in. Unbelieving, inexperienced in disaster, I had stood my ground and seen catastrophe, a vast grey wall of water, monstrous, unnatural, rise in the distance and crash fast as lightning towards me and beyond me, its heavy muffled roar the mad indifferent voice of Nature that I had never heard before. Tidal wave. Labour pains. Both natural, both quite indifferent to the fragile splinters of humanity that lay in their paths. A nut caught in the nutcracker.

When pain ended, I lay on one elbow and regarded my child. The nurse gave me a booklet, ornamented with sketches of flowers and baby birds. There were poems inside, about little strangers and violets and pink and blue and, above all, about love. They bore no relation to what I was feeling because I was feeling nothing. A vacuum of immense proportions had replaced the foetus, my bruised womb was distended with it. Numb, anaesthetized, I stared over vast distances at this small creature lying on my pillow and I could not think that it belonged to me.

That sense of distance continued. The baby and I were two strangers booked into the same compartment of a train, two prisoners locked into the same cell. I would sit at one end of the sofa, he, a shawled bundle, would lie propped at the opposite end and we would regard each other. I stared a lot at that baby as if he were the last piece in a Chinese puzzle and, by staring, I might suddenly see where he fitted to make a whole. If only I could somehow turn him and tip him carefully enough, I could finally slot him into an intricate jigsaw, put him away in a drawer with other discarded games and get on with my life again.

Everyone who came through our door seemed to love my infant. They cooed, they snuffled, their arms automatically reached out to enfold him. They breathed in deeply as if he were a fragrance, their eyes shone. My eyes did not shine, my arms were stiff, I did not coo or even speak. The baby and I, when they left, were stranded together again. I was so lonely I feared I no longer existed and the baby was merely an ingredient of that loneliness, part of it. I thought him lonely too. He certainly looked it, a chick left in the nest, purblind and helpless, twitching a little, staring sightlessly at the blank oval that was my face.

Day after day I searched, fumbling inside myself to find a piece of love. Where is it, where is it, I know it's supposed to be there, it was put there especially, they told me so. And, not finding it, I felt so sad for him, for the child. It was supposed to be for him, after all. They said it would come when he came, but evidently they had failed to send it or it had been mislaid. I cried for him, the poor unlucky scrap.

Later, with two more children, love did not materialize or, if it did, I was simply too busy to recognize it. Woken abruptly every morning to the cries of hungry children, I felt they were taking all the air in the house, there was none left for me to breathe. Their demands filled every hour, they were the flood conjured by the sorcerer's apprentice and I was the apprentice, rushing from pillar to post merely to be freshly inundated. Others, visiting, saw them pretty and small. To me they were vast, swollen creatures intent on my downfall. They were giants and I was Tom Thumb, sheltering from huge bodies that threatened my annihilation. I had nightmares about them, I was oddly frightened of them. In the evening I would hear a noise at the door and my heart rattling in my chest I would imagine that on the stair stood an infant in long nightdress and nappies, six feet tall, its spreading mouth clamped over a great dummy, and at the sight my hair would whiten and I would instantly go mad. Goodness knows where love had got to. By this time I had given up the idea of its existence and steeled myself to manage without it, manage these great infants as best I could.

Was this, then, motherhood? The source of all love, the image of love's perfection upon which all future loves would be based? God help us all.

Luckily for me and them, love did eventually grow and flourish. The slowness of its germination had to do, I think, with the overriding myth of love at first sight. Everyone conspired to make me believe that one look at my newborn would generate instant, undying and undiluted love and therefore, when this didn't happen, I despaired of myself and the baby. I was never told that though love may be immediate it is often not so. I was never told, either, that love has its time as much as life and death, so that a woman may find it hard to love babies and easy to love the growing child, or that if she has not yet learned to love herself, she cannot properly love others.

I learned this because love grew slowly for the first children and was instant and complete with the last, born five years after the rest. This one was not an accidental happening, a growth in my belly that I had not wished, at a time I would not have chosen. This one was a purpose-built baby, wanted before pregnancy ever materialized and a pleasure to carry. I was ready myself, secure enough, familiar enough with my own character, to turn outwards to another human being without the constant fear of earlier days that a baby would take away what I still badly needed for myself.

So he was born and to me became the sun, warming the parts that other children did not reach. Through him, I learnt how to love to the best of my ability. Tending him while he was small my well-inflated ego, perfectly obvious in my dealings with the rest of the world, became invisible. His good was paramount, not in any sacrificial sense but because I myself was not at ease unless he was. There was never any question of putting my needs first because his needs were my needs. In those early years he felt, to me, an extension of my body, an extra limb. When I cared for him I cared for me. When he and I were in a room together, it was as if I were alone. I knew, for the first time, that if anything happened that demanded my death to save him, I would take that action automatically. Courage, self-sacrifice were merely words that in no way reflected my state of mind. Simply, it would be easier to die for him than to live, knowing him dead. I loved him not better than myself, but as myself.

I did not invoke this feeling by any effort and there was no morality in it. It was. And it lasted as long as he needed it. Slowly, he grew separate, slowly, day by day, he signalled that separateness and we drew away from each other. Our once one-flesh divided again, sealing me into me, him into him. He is now a teenager and, as it happens, as different from me in every characteristic, physical and mental, as can well be imagined of a mother and her offspring. Since his young childhood, we have experienced together the whole spectrum of emotion – anger, irritation, indifference, pleasure, dislike, interest, joy and plain boredom. But that purely physical bond remains and, I imagine, will always remain. He is my flesh and as unlovable and uninteresting as that. You do not feel emotion for your own flesh. Mostly, you have no conscious feeling about it at all.

I know, though, that quite without my own volition, this early love of mine gave him almost all he will ever need in life. He has a confidence, an unshakeable appreciation of his own worth that is almost laughably without any source in his actual abilities. At times, this solid inner core has irritated the hell out of me. I have shouted and cursed at him, told him I think him a fool and a nincompoop, tried, in fury, to break down that wall that I myself built, but he is invincible, a rock, pure granite. Outside, he may wail, cry, be depressed, look anxious. Inside him is the eye of the hurricane where the air is calm, the essence that is himself. I could not have given him that by effort alone. No amount of conscientious work would have formed it. Like chicken-pox, my own feeling infected him. And I am sure that out of that steady core of love he, in his time, will infect another. He

37

was born knowing what love was, what it felt like, the furniture of it, the comfort of it, the absoluteness of it and though that in no way guarantees his future happy love life, because adult love demands other ingredients, it does guarantee that he will always know it when he finds it because it will be familiar, like coming home.

I had my first three children before I was twenty-five and with a man I did not love. I could not put my self aside in their interests because I had not yet found a self to put aside. Out there, beyond my door, the world shone and glinted, a great roundabout. The children caught at my skirts and tugged me back, I tugged away, their needs and mine were opposite. On one level my needs were frivolous enough – pretty clothes, loud music, bright lights, admiring eyes, but all these things meant people and people were my real craving. How to know who you are without catching sight of your reflection in someone else's eyes? I yearned for a hall of mirrors to see myself lovely but, failing that, to see myself in any way at all, tall or small, fat or thin, plain or ugly. Instead I was imprisoned in a kitchen without reflections, four walls cut me off from movement, every day dawned with its inexorable routine and answered not a one of my cravings. I was a robot designed for washing nappies, a machine for making up bottles. Fury continually rose inside me, guilt forced it back for a while, the to-ing and fro-ing exhausted me. I was not nice to be near, I was in no way a mother, I was in no way a person.

And all this turmoil, this lack of love, was a result only of mental anguish, a psychological insecurity, a hunger for identity and a fear of inner loss. Physically, all was well. I was healthy, active, well-fed, and able to provide the same material comfort for my children. Yet love between us did not come easily. How much less easily must it have come for my distaff ancestor, deprived of all those material comforts, for whom every day and every hour was a battle for survival, a battle whose odds were tipped more heavily against her whenever there was a new infant mouth to feed. My children threatened my mental security. Hers often threatened life itself.

My last child was born nine years after the first and a lot had happened in those years. I had made many conscious decisions. Left a husband, met another, moved countries, suffered grief and joy, learnt the hard comfort of work, the strains and satisfactions of a growing independence in thought and economics. I knew something of who I was and accepting it, good and bad, stood more firmly on my feet. Now, I could afford to stretch out a hand to my new infant. Out of my own self-knowledge I understood something of what he needed and was able to give it to him, from my better-stocked shelves. What little I know of maternal love came then. It was a long way from perfect but it was, for the first time, there.

The usual theories of the source of maternal love lead back to the mother's own upbringing. It is assumed that if she was loved by her parents, she will love her children in her turn. Obviously, a child reared without love is damaged. Unfamiliar with the trappings of love, the adult may neither recognize it nor inspire it. Psychologists explain psychopaths, those a-loving people, as grown-up children whom no one ever loved. The psychopath learned early that no-love was the climate of life and, in the continuing struggle for survival, substituted the manipulation of others to provide some transient warmth. Inside him is a vacuum, cold as space, but pretence of feeling is easy enough and winning enough to succeed. Sometimes the psychopath, steaming like dry ice, kills, perhaps in fury at the vacuum inside, perhaps in a ghastly hope of filling it. Surveys of battering mothers come again and again to the same conclusions – the mother herself was a product of a battering home or was colossally neglected, an unloved scrap of humanity that, grown, cannot manage the last straw of a child. Usually, too, battering mothers are very young, formed by a childish misery that remains undiluted by any later experience.

Love in childhood is clearly important but it is not all. Later learning, the search for the self, is equally important. If childhood experience had been the absolute criterion, then I – and a host of others like me – would have behaved in the same way to all our children. The female monkey, deprived of parents at birth, is unable to be maternal to any of her offspring. I, on the other hand, am a less programmed animal and though the first learning process has an effect, it is only part of a continuing lesson, a continual unfolding that is not innate, though perhaps genetically triggered. As a human being I had to discover myself, learn my place among other individuals, before I could give love out.

I do not know how much, or how little, my own initial lack of love may have damaged my first children. God knows, I meant well but I could not make the soufflé because I had no eggs. The last child inhaled my love with his first breath, because by that time I had found the eggs. Or enough of them to do.

So it has been for most of history. That evidence of maternal love upon which all later love rests its case, when questioned by the prosecution, turns out not to have been there at the time, or to have been there but asleep or deaf, or preoccupied with other things.

From the wreckage we can salvage one fact. To care for offspring is, in many species, instinctual, one part of the survival kit that is labelled 'the show must go on'. A stickleback may fight to the death to defend its baby stickleback but the imperative is racial and not personal. If father stickleback later, absent-mindedly, swallows a son or a daughter, he does not notice the loss. A mother bird, trailing a wing to lure enemies away from her nestlings, is programmed by Nature to risk her life for theirs but not to recognize those nestlings once they have flown.

Among such species there is no such thing as 'good' or 'bad' mothering and no youngsters grow into adults damaged by the bad and so unable to fulfil their own parenting tasks. That fate is reserved for the more complex creatures and, most of all, for us. Discarding the certainty of instinctual behaviour, we took an evolutionary gamble on the frontiers of learning. De-programmed, we plumped for a DIY world that extracted awesome penalties for failure but offered as reward the possibilities of adaptability, change and progress.

For most of our history most of us have been poor, hard-worked and ignorant and therefore mothering has been a hit-and-miss affair, good enough to populate the earth but basically unconnected with the individual child – a tight enough bond to promote survival but too constricting for the child's inner growth or for the growth of a love that meets those needs. In many ways, the undifferentiated feelings of the mother for her child worked out well enough. She wished to survive, the child was part of her; if she managed, she managed for them both. But if conditions for survival were tough, if life itself was a daily battle for food and shelter, as it has been for thousands of years for the vast majority of people, then children were just another of life's arbitrary events, sometimes a threat to the parents' survival, sometimes – as in agricultural societies to this day – a kind of bonus in the shape of extra hands.

But to look to motherhood throughout the centuries for the secret, the source and the mainspring of true adult love is to look in vain. The cradle is empty, the child crippled, the hope lies elsewhere, in future learning. One day, conditions being right, we may fill cradles with children who all inherit at birth the new love now painfully wrested by a few parents from a personal and hard-won experience.

THREE

The Toll

'Oh, see what love has done to me.'

Femme est secours contre faiblesse
Joie contre melancolie
Sens et avis contre folie
Courtoisie contre rudesse
Elle est terrestre paradis . . .

Presumably because women are the mothers of the race, love in all its aspects is considered to be our natural habitat. Like medicine, we are to be taken by men as an antidote for their melancholy, madness, brutality and, as the unknown medieval French poet wrote, to provide for them an earthly paradise. 'Try a little tenderness,' sang Frank Sinatra, as if he were advocating that men learn a foreign language. 'Man's love is of man's life a thing apart; 'Tis woman's whole existence,' said Lord Byron, explaining a primitive tribe to the civilized. Women, says the world, are the loving ones and we say it, too. We clean and love, we cook and love, we sew and love, we make love and love. We love men killing each other on battlefields, kittens starving in gutters, demagogues shouting from balconies, gurus praying in ashrams, pop stars waving from planes, squat tycoons loud with diamonds, gangsters who kiss and kill, poets in garrets, actors in photographs, pimps who steal from us and beat us up, murderers, terrorists, alcoholics, sadists, sunsets, stars, moons, Junes and baby birds with broken wings.

We are, in other words, love-logged sponges for soothing and scrubbing off the dirt of a dirty world. All that is required of us is a soft bosom, cool hands, a quiet voice, easy tears and the soggiest of bleeding hearts.

Lord Byron's aphorism is usually taken as a wise and perceptive comment on the way things are, but it is also the way it suited men for things to be. Love was a woman's whole existence because she was allowed no other and, besides, if a man is going to have you cooking and cleaning and nursing and feeding him it is much nicer for him to believe that you do it for love. That's all right then, he can think, buffing his fingernails, flicking fluff from his lapel and smiling into the mirror before he goes off into the real world. She does it because she loves me and she loves loving me.

Indeed, so convenient has love been for men that sometimes it is impossible to avoid the thought that they invented it, exuded it like spiders, a silky floss, to be woven into a sticky web so that they could squat at the corners and wait for the female fly. What a beautiful thing, says the little lady passing by, dazzled at the gleaming threads, but the spider does not think so. He keeps his limbs meticulously free of his incidental artwork and waits patiently to catch the useful, tasty fly. The spider, my dear, knows what's what. The web is of his life a thing apart. 'Tis the fly's fate, poor foolish fly.

It is, in fact, a wonder of the world that loving has not extinguished the female of the species and left the men to inherit a monosex earth, preserving one last female footprint before the sex became extinct, love-bloated dinosaurs with little brains who fell victim long ago to some burning cataclysm of Nature known to the twentieth century only by a layer of cinders in a rock. We are the loving ones, love is expendable, we are expendable. As it happens, we have survived until now through profligacy – though we die for love, Nature has always made sure we linger long enough to reproduce ourselves and another before we bow out. Love is a queendom colonized by men and in the Governor's Palace, women scrub the floors.

If you do not believe me, think on these things.

Who are the authorities on love, the writers of guidebooks through that territory? Men. Almost all the philosophy, the etiquette, the poetry, the manuals and the analyses of love through history are male-invented and male-edited, though they all direct their edicts to women as their pupils. So masculine, indeed, is the history of love that a Martian, examining our literature, would assume it to be a purely male emotion, testament to the sensitivity and aspirations of one sex's soul. When women do come into it they distinctly lower the tone, they seem unable to rise to the proper heights and are frequently admonished for their failure. The male proprietary note is constant, he invented love, he owns it, he alone truly appreciates its finer points and, alas, he has no proper subject upon whom to try out his invention except coarse-grained women. His solution throughout history is very clear – he has pretended to love women and has, in fact, aimed at quite different targets, like any soldier who, practising violent death, sticks a straw dummy in place of the longed-for enemy.

As far back as the twelfth and thirteenth centuries, in that little French kingdom of Angevin which is so often credited as the birthplace of romantic love and where, for a brief time, love did indeed seem to rule, and with it, women, the surface difference turns out, upon closer examination, to be just that, a surface. In spite of the Courts of Love set up by high-born ladies and the whole ethic which put women on a high and distant pedestal to be worshipped by their male vassals, the structure merely camouflaged other and quite different goals. Those *belles dames* who believed themselves so adored, who thought their favours were all men desired, were, as was so often to happen, fooled. They imagined that they made the rules but, in reality, they were mere puppets manipulated by men in search of other ends.

What exactly those ends were has provoked much argument. Some say that the entire panoply of courtly love, with all its meticulous rituals, codes of behaviour and even vocabulary, was invented as an elaborate disguise for warring religious factions, as a cover for the old heretic religions in the face of a Christian take-over. Women, happily blinded by the sudden gift of superficial power, thought themselves the centre of attention and were only the red herrings, carefully set up to distract attention from the real game. Some explain the phenomenon in terms of man's quest for a heightened reality which could only be achieved by using death to spice life. The women, led to believe that every order they gave would be obeyed, were pushed by men's wishes into issuing the orders men most wanted – orders to face death by any means, from a crusade in foreign and dangerous lands to the domestic tournaments that risked life and limb. Men jousted with death and pretended they did it for women. And the women, hoodwinked by vanity and by a rush of apparent equality to the head, never realized the one consistent and obvious outcome of their puppet commands – that they gave the male lover the permission he had so assiduously angled for, to absent himself from his so-called beloved, in the name of an absolute obedience to her wishes. Off he went for years at a time to the Crusades or on a variety of impossible adventures, breathing a sigh of relief at having manipulated his Lady cleverly enough to purchase his absence with honour. And there she sat in her castle tower, a grass mistress waiting for her lover's return, blithely unaware that she had just been handed love's greatest insult, the desire of her Knight to be anywhere else but with her.

Nor were things a lot better when he was there. The only effective principle of love in Anjou was the separation of lovers, an aberration thought up and put into practice by men who believed that their own greater spiritual good would result; that by absence or abstinence they were laying up treasures in heaven. This involved two imperatives. The woman must already be married to someone else, thus making ultimate unity impossible, and – on a more basic level – she must not be sexually possessed. 'Donnoi' was the Provençal word for the vassal relationship set up between a knight-lover and his lady or Domina and the ethos behind it is summed up by the Donnoi edict, 'He knows truly nothing who wants fully to possess his Lady'. In the great drama of Tristan and Iseult which so effectively mirrors that ancient society, Tristan is so determined never to possess Iseult that even when they are at last alone in a clearing in the forest, able finally to consummate their love, Tristan draws his sword and puts it between them, clearly symbolizing that despite all his travails to win Iseult the one thing he does not wish is for the travails to end, thus illustrating his true feeling – 'tis more entertaining to travel than to arrive. Tristan, like all his masculine peers and progeny, preferred the extreme excitation of being hopelessly in love to the consummation thereof. He was, in crude twentieth-century terms, not a lover but a wanker. Denis de Rougemont in *Passion and Society* says of him:

Tristan wanted the branding of love more than he wanted Iseult, for he believed that the intense and devouring flame of passion would make him divine, the equal of the world. Passion requires that the self shall become greater than all things, as solitary and powerful as God.

And in this, Tristan represented all his contemporaries who could afford to spare the time for such frivolities. Iseult was left to sum up, sadly, the bleak truth: 'Il ne m'aime pas, ne je lui.'

Women paid a high price for this pseudo-adoration. Not only did they find that the result of their participation in this male game was inevitably their desertion by eager and apparently submissive lovers, a desertion that left them alone with the husbands who regarded them merely as chattels, but they must also have been aware, however dimly, that the other side of adoration was all too frequently hatred and fear. The general medieval view of woman was that she represented the supreme temptress, the *janua diaboli*, the greatest of all obstacles to salvation, and though the cult of the Virgin Mary flourished alongside this fear and hatred, the Mother of God in her purity and sexlessness simply emphasized the sins of every other woman not so appointed. The convents of the time were the only respectable refuges for women, whether married or unmarried, because only there, confined and limited, could women obtain any approbation for their existence.

Under all the elaborate ritual and gloriously embroidered pictures made by men of lovely, capricious, merciless women, ordinary females eked out their existence, hardworking and often loaded with heavy responsibilities. While the men decimated themselves in wars and feuds and refused to reproduce themselves in vows of monkish celibacy, women worked and widows took over their dead husbands' trades. Hardly a trade or craft or business was without a goodly complement of women. The *Book of Crafts of Etienne Boileau*, drawn up in the last half of the thirteenth century, lists a hundred crafts flourishing in Paris, all of them practised by women and at least five run solely by them. While the troubadours sang and the poets penned lays to their own female inventions, real women carried on with the real work of life, hampered by male frivolities but not paralyzed.

And who are the *dramatis personae* whose line stretches back through history, players in this odd one-sided game called love? A vast horde of men, too numerous to list all but a few. The Greeks: Ovid with his *Ars Amatoria*, Plato on non-sexual love between men, politely widened today to include women. The Greco-Romans: Plutarch, Petronius, Lucian, Apuleius. A host of Arabs including the eleventh-century philospher Avicenna. The French, who produced the first troubadour, Guillaume, Count of Poitou; the 'veritable love breviary' *Roman de la Rose*, begun in 1240 by Guillaume de Lorris and completed forty years later by Jean de Meun; and between the twelfth and fourteenth centuries, a deluge of far more didactic manuals of love that were mostly disguised etiquette books with careful rules for the one hundred and one things a woman should do.

Andreas Capellanus, chaplain to Philip II, wrote his *Liber de Arte Honesti Amandi* at the end of the twelfth century. Though it had some nice insouciant thoughts ('the excuse of marriage cannot be invoked against love'), the chaplain's true feelings leak out in Book Three, where he abuses love (for which, read 'women') for causing men to eat less, drink less and become bodily weak, with bad digestion, fevers and numberless other ills including galloping senility. 'Any man,' he says towards the end of his treatise, 'who devotes his efforts to love, loses all usefulness.' Thirteenth-century love manuals are even more specifically directed at the errant female sex. Jacques d'Amiens enjoins cleanliness, politeness, discretion, coquetry and the necessity for women to be young, beautiful and accomplished for men's entertainment. Brother Ermengau's *Breviari d'amor* stresses a knowledge of etiquette and, rather contradictorily, honesty. Richard de Fournival instructs ladies, in *Cousans d'amor*, to be humble, truthful, loyal, gracious and generous. In the late thirteenth century the Italians joined the fray with their Stilnovisti school of poets – Guinicelli, Cavalcanti, Dante – all writing of women too angelic ever to be possessed.

And so they proceed through the years, from Petrarch to Chaucer, from anonymous Egyptian male scribes to the English milords Halifax and Chesterfield of the seventeenth and eighteenth centuries, admonishing fingers wagging, intent either on elevating their ladies out of sight or keeping docile female pupils under their thumbs, those females for whom, alone, the lessons of love were intended. Men, after all, had better things to do.

Besides lecturing in love, men were also the myth-makers. In their stories of Ancient Greece, love brought women disasters on an appropriately Olympian scale. Shepherdess or nymph, earthly beauty or heavenly goddess, few emerge from the experience in anything but disarray and most suffer cosmic calamities. Echo falls in love with Narcissus and, since he was already in love with himself, pines away in grief until she becomes merely a noise in a tunnel. And any unfortunate female who fancied Zeus not only had to contend with Hera's jealous rage but, worse, her lover's amatory games. Leda is made pregnant by Zeus the Swan and gives birth to two eggs; Europa is raped by Zeus the Bull; Leto wanders the earth looking for a refuge to bear her son by Zeus and is constantly turned away for fear of Hera's anger; Io is turned into a heifer by jealous Hera, who also sends a gad-fly to torment her and drive her frenziedly from land to land, and poor Metis has the child taken out of her body by Zeus in case she bears a son to supplant him. There is a morality tale for women, too, in the myth of Psyche, the hapless princess who falls in love with Love himself, and dares to turn the light on and peek at him. He upbraids her for her action and flees, leaving the wretched lady to trek from temple to temple looking for him. Arriving at the palace of Aphrodite, Goddess of Love, her miseries really begin. She is treated as a slave, given the harshest and most humiliating chores, and would die except that Cupid – who has taken up with her again – helps her and eventually reconciles her with Aphrodite. At last she becomes immortal and is united with her lover. Since Psyche represents the soul, the Grecian moral is clear: only via the purification of suffering can human beings reach true happiness. Or, to put it more clearly, women must suffer for love while men sit around giving them a nudge in the right direction. *Oi vey.*

Sadder still, myths are often quite mild versions of the actual penalties women had to pay for love, a harsh and frequently lethal payment. Traditionally, the institution of marriage had little, if anything, to do with love and, since most women had to marry in order to exist and, once married, were virtually and sometimes literally imprisoned for life, many of them may never have experienced any emotion approaching love at all. Even today, many girls devote so much of their time, money, dreams and thoughts to the marriage ceremony itself (around which, in response, a huge industry has been built up) that men have sometimes labelled them unromantic. I remember a cartoon in an American magazine that captured this male view: a couple dreaming, cheek to cheek under a tree, he of the approved hearts and flowers, she of washing machines, nappies and prams. In fact, these girls are sadly practical – though they may talk otherwise, they know only too well that their wedding day may be all of love they ever have to cherish. Lee Comer in *Wedlocked Women* writes:

For many girls their fantasies revolve not around the man of their dreams but around the dress, the flowers, the hymns, the guests and present list, the bridesmaids and the speeches and the whole display that attends the ritual . . . The wedding is the culmination of all that the girl has been conditioned to believe about herself. She hands over her identity to her husband in exchange for a small portion of his, she takes his name and promises to love, honour and obey and she listens while the vicar pronounces them, not 'husband and wife', not 'man and woman' but 'man and wife'. The ritualistic incantation of these words which define her inferior status not in the eyes of God but in the eyes of the world, must be accompanied by as much physical adornment as possible. This is the *real* purpose of the display – the long white cover-all dress, the face hidden by a

49

veil and the bent head ... the more beautiful she looks in this disguise, the more profuse are the tears. We weep for joy. Will she ever again know such happiness as she has known on this, her greatest day? Probably not.

Will she ever, indeed, experience love at all? Probably not.

In some ways, all these heart-whole women were fortunate. Those who fancied others than their husbands and dared to express it through adultery or far less – a sigh, a tear, an incriminating letter – showed the most awesome courage in the face of horrifying penalties. To forestall such loving expression, medieval husbands trussed their wives in chastity belts, heavy iron girdings that can be seen in museums, have become a music-hall joke and must have been, to the sad lady, a continuous minor torture, rubbing soft skin into suppuration, accumulating filth, a weighty and interminable reminder that her master cared not a whit that her heart was not his as long as her body was, and that only to ensure that no child be sired upon her by a rival.

Adultery in most cultures carried the death penalty and that only after trials by horror. While troubadours sang of ladies fair, *dames lointaines, belles et sans merci,* while castle balconies echoed to ballads praising feminine delicacy, beauty, fragility, the woman who foolishly allowed herself to be persuaded by such soft talk was savaged by another man, her husband, with the full approval of the laws of the land. One lady, who embalmed her dead lover's heart, was forced to eat it. Another was given for rape to a wandering band of lepers. The early Middle Ages were pretty well open season on adulteresses and what evidence we have shows that men vied with each other to find the most ingenious and original punishments. Already in fifth-century Burgundy both lovers were condemned to death under the Code. Another law, included in a thirteenth-century Spanish code, ordained that the adulteress be given to the adulterer's wife, to revenge herself as she would. Other women had their heads shaved and were driven nude through the streets, imprisoned for long periods and forced to wear armbands to publicize their sin.

Nor were the Middle Ages unique or even especially cruel in the punishment of adultery. In Ancient Greece, an adulteress might not adorn herself or mingle with and corrupt other women. If she did, any passing male was encouraged to tear off her garment and beat her, 'so that her life may be not worth living'. In fact, the law ordained that she might suffer any maltreatment short of death. She was, of course, automatically repudiated by her husband and a father too had the power to kill his adulterous daughter until the third century AD. Female slaves were below the law; nothing protected them from any sort of cruelty. In early Rome men briefly lost the power to kill their wives and daughters-in-law, though Marcus Cato the Elder maintained that husbands had the 'natural' right to kill wives taken in adultery, without trial, while if the husband himself commits adultery, his wife 'must not presume to lay a finger on you, nor does the law allow it'. Later Julian Law set out meticulous lists of classes of men a husband or father might kill as adulterers, provided that the adulteress was first dispatched – if she was not, then the man's death was deemed murder. A woman might be lucky enough only to lose half of her dowry, a third of her estates and be exiled to an island nunnery. If she, as a freedwoman, had loved a slave, he was burned and she was put to death.

Byzantine law decreed that an adulteress should have her nose slit and be forced into professional whoredom. The early Hebrew fathers punished adultery with death by stoning 'to rid Israel of this wickedness'. Islam shut adulteresses up for life, first stoning married women and flogging the unmarried as fornicators, a practice still carried out in parts of Islam today. From Palermo to Budapest to Calais, a man who caught his wife *in flagrante* might kill her on the spot, a sentence that still survives in the indulgent handling of the *crime passionnel*.

In *Love and the French* Nina Epton tells the story of a lady who absconded with her lover and was condemned to imprisonment in the Convent of the Cordelières, to have her head shaved and don the religious habit for a period of three years, during which time her husband was allowed to visit her and 'enjoy' conjugal relations. The abbess of the convent was to administer discipline by beating her three times a month. The lady's lover went scot-free.

Nina Epton adds the history of a husband who killed his

wife's lover and then had his bones set in an aumbry which his wife was compelled to contemplate daily. Her hair was cut short, she was made to live in retirement and to drink out of her dead lover's skull. Later, the King put in a word for her, she was forgiven and 'bore her husband a numerous progeny'. One is tempted to wonder which punishment she considered the worse.

In the turmoil of the Renaissance and the Reformation, court ladies, at least, improved their lot and some male writers began to defend them against the worst male excesses. The education of rich women became more prevalent though the general feeling was summed up by Erasmus's Abbot Antronius who was against education for women 'because it contributes nothing towards the defence of their chastity'. As Protestantism began to make itself felt it was Luther who decided that adultery was a ground for divorce. His follower, John Calvin, used the threat of hellfire as a more effective deterrent than earthly punishment and further narrowed already rigid sexual confines by ordaining that chastity was best, and marriage was indicated for those who could not manage this extreme, and even within it there was to be no unbridled lust. The man, he said, who abuses marriage by lecherous intemperance is committing adultery with his own wife. And the German Dominican monk, Martin Bucer, stoutly maintained that always and ever the only true punishment for female adultery was death.

The black tidal wave of witch-hunting in Europe rose to its ghastly peaks after the first stirrings of emancipation during the Renaissance, a fearful backlash brought on, according to Hugh Trevor-Roper, by the 'frontal opposition of Catholics and Protestants', a religious war that 'sent men back to the old dualism of God and the Devil and the hideous reservoir of hatred which seemed to be drying up, was suddenly refilled'. The writers of that witch-hunters' handbook, *Malleus Maleficarum*, set the scene with a fine double-bind that neatly condemned all women as possible witches because 'all witchcraft comes from carnal lust, which is in women insatiable'. Men like Jean Bodin, Reginald Scot and the Dominican inquisitors hastened to agree, vying with each other to express their disgust and abhorrence for women with all the queasiness of stomach so typical of their ilk – the female was to them bestial, brutish, fickle, bloody, foul-smelling, suppurating, belching, infectious, full of evil humours and pernicious excrements.

Now, women could be punished for adultery with living men *and* with the Devil, though the penalties for the imaginary sexual congress were the harshest – fire, the noose, the ducking-stool and a myriad horrid tortures beforehand. 'There is,' said a witness of the time, 'no limit of duration or severity or repetition of the tortures.' Altogether, some nine million women were executed as witches over three centuries, the infection spread to the New World in the seventeenth century and two villages in France survived the holocaust with a female population of one each. 'Poor doting women', the inquisitor Scot called them, and certainly the hysterics that led to suspicion of diabolic possession could well have had to do with love starvation.

Because of our own experience in sex today, we are forced to wonder whether the terrible risks that adulterous women ran were ever actually compensated in, at the very least, physical pleasure. It seems unlikely. Since little was then known about women's bodies or sexuality and the clitoris was a rare *trouvaille*; since men were hardly adept at arousing their mistresses and women conditioned not to mention to their lovers what little they might have discovered about their own feelings; and since most women must have been anxious about the possible pregnancy that would give the game away, the chances of much physical pleasure seem slim. Of course we should not fall into the trap of imagining even the history of the orgasm as a slow upward spiral towards the twentieth century or assume that, because Victorian women were severely discouraged from any admission of sexuality, so it was with all women before them, yet all the indications are that the orgasm was not a usual reward for the risks of adultery. Today, in this permissive society which has removed most of the outward guilts and pressures from sexual intercourse, the surveys still show that more women do not experience orgasm than do and the pre-orgasmic group, aimed at teaching women how to experience orgasm, is spreading from America even to the Old World. Whereas one thing we know about men is that, in sex, ejaculation is almost a *sine qua non*, even if the pleasure is marred in some other way, it is possible that many women's only outlet for the nervous excitation of sexual energy was masturbation. If the images that were summoned up during this solitary exercise were distinctly godly or diabolically devilish, they would only confirm the woman's own belief in her possession by a God or a demon.

At the end of the witch hunts, in the Age of Enlightenment, canon law decreed that adultery was as reprehensible for a husband as for a wife. Nevertheless, it was the wife who lost her dowry and her lands, was locked into a convent for life and still risked violent death – the only real deterrent to the husband being that he might not, by murdering his wife, profit by her money.

And so the double standard marched on, as it still does in our day. Madame de Pompadour told the story of the Countess d'Egmont – young, lovely and rich – who was visited by her mother's confessor and informed that she was the fruit of an adultery her mother had been trying to expiate for twenty-five years. The confessor insisted that she could save her mother's soul only by refusing marriage and entering a nunnery. The Countess complied. The sins of the mother shall be visited upon the daughter. The sins of the father shall not be visited at all.

And then, in the eighteenth century, dawned the age of the French Salon, well-born women's first attempt to find themselves an individual identity. Traditionally merely disposed in marriage like brood mares brought to stud, these ladies were now permitted to enjoy an intellectual relationship with an admirer and toy with the possibility that, though the body was pre-empted by the husband, the heart could be given elsewhere. Love became an elegant game, a way to assert personality and power, however fleetingly. 'Among us,' said Mademoiselle de Scudéry, a *saloneuse* and novelist of the time, 'love is not a simple passion as it is elsewhere, it is one of the requirements of good breeding.

Every lady must be loved ... the honour of our beauties consists in keeping the slaves they have made by the sheer power of their attractions and not by according favours.' The women who practised this disembodied art were sneeringly called 'Les Précieuses' by men who preferred earthier pleasures, and the precious ones may well have been irritatingly fey at times; but their idea of a tender friendship between men and women was something quite new, a brave revolt against male tyranny, within marriage and without, and several of them did inspire lifelong devotion from their *tendres amis.* Saint-Évremond pronounced upon them: 'If you wish to know the greatest claim to merit of the Précieuses, I shall tell you that it was in tenderly loving their lovers without sex and getting solid sexual satisfaction from their husbands while disliking them.' For the ladies' sakes, we can but hope he was right.

Later, as Platonic love went out of fashion, sex entered the Salons – adultery became not only *à la mode* but was, among the rich and well-born, considered a most absorbing occupation. Among ordinary people, however, adultery continued to be a crime for which a woman could be discarded by her husband, automatically stripped of all her property and possessions and disgraced in the eyes of the community. When Queen Victoria ascended the English throne, married her Albert and continued to worship his memory throughout her long widowhood, she set a one-woman standard of claustrophobic marital love that bore little or no relation to the fact that women were still considered marriageable chattels, to be passed from father to husband without consideration of their own emotions. Hypocrisy in love reached new heights and adultery by wives commanded to adore their husbands was punished by the cruellest legalistic devices and social disgrace. Poor Caroline Norton, granddaughter of Richard Brinsley Sheridan, was accused by her husband of what was discreetly called 'criminal conversation', held up to public ridicule and deprived of her only child. This was at a time when masculine extra-marital delights were never more prevalent; prostitution, including child prostitution, flourished and the most perverse of pornography commanded high prices. The rigidity of Victorian marriage and the impossibility of living outside it with a lover certainly gave rise to the *grand guignol* parade of Victorian murderesses who killed implacable husbands in desperate attempts to free themselves for the other man.

Yet in spite of the severity of its penalties, adultery was only one among the miseries and tribulations endured by women in the name of love. The fury of a male-dominated world was directed at the adulterous wife not out of jealousy for the loss of her love but the fear that she would conceive a bastard child to pollute the husband's lineage, and so she often did – how could she not, in those pre-pill days? It is a matter for wonder that women ever dared have a physical relationship with a lover at all, so awesome and inevitable were the risks of pregnancy, disgrace, the death of the child and the death of the mother herself. Even if a woman were lucky enough to love her own husband, the price she paid for love's physical consummation, endless pregnancies, lacked only the disgrace accorded her less fortunate sister.

It may be that, further back in time, pregnancy was not so inevitably an outcome of sex. There is evidence that women once knew of herbal contraceptives or were so attuned to their own sexual rhythms that unwanted pregnancies did not occur – in some tribal societies it has been observed that no girl becomes pregnant before marriage, despite the fact that sexual intercourse between unmarried young people is permissible and frequent. There are indications, too, that before men conceived of property and the woman as part of that property, childbirth was not the continuous ordeal it would later become. When men could not claim absolute jurisdiction over a woman's body, then that woman had some control over her own reproduction, some room for manoeuvre. If all else failed, she needed only to avoid men in order to rest her body. Anthropologists report many examples of this practice, often emphasized by laws, among prehistoric and primitive peoples. The Akikuyu are polygamous, a clan of women and children who show no jealousy towards each other's relations with the headman and are free to present themselves for sex when they wish. Among the Southern Bantu peoples, sex is strictly forbidden until the second or third year after the birth of a child and this taboo is duplicated in many tribes for varying times. But with the dawn of 'civilization' and patriarchy, woman lost this simple right and biology became her destiny with a vengeance. Later, when men took over medicine, excluded the midwife and female relatives and constructed the hospital as a male domain for the practice of male medicine, the penalties for an act of love or sex grew ever harsher.

Parish records, historic documents and ancient tombstones all attest to this. Scratch away the mould and the moss and, more often than not, you will find a man's name and listed underneath the earlier dates of his deceased first, second and third wives, often buried with the newborn infants that caused their deaths. Gregorio Dati, a Florentine merchant of the fourteenth century, records in his accounting books (along with other business) the travails of his four wives:

My beloved wife, Bandecca, went to Paradise after a nine-month illness started by a miscarriage, July 1390. I had an illegitimate child by Margherita, a Tartar slave whom I had bought.

He marries again.

On Sunday, 17 May 1394, Betta gave birth to a girl.
On Friday evening, 17 March 1396, the Lord blessed our marriage with a male son.
12 March 1397 Betta gave birth to our third child.
27 April 1398, Betta gave birth to our fourth child.
1 July 1399, Betta had our fifth child.
22 June 1400, Betta gave birth for the sixth time.
On Wednesday, 13 July 1401 the Lord lent us a seventh child.
On 5 July 1402 Betta gave birth to our eighth child.
After that my wife Betta passed on to Paradise.

Gregorio is betrothed a year later, married the year after that and his wife Ginevra produces eleven children.

After that it was God's will to recall to Himself the blessed soul of my wife Ginevra. She died in childbirth after lengthy suffering.

He marries again and the new wife miscarries within four

months. She then produces five children in as many years and Gregorio stops keeping his book, fatigued, perhaps, by so many entries.

Mrs Alice Thornton, a Yorkshire lady who lived in the seventeenth century, herself records milestones not a whit less bleak for the intervening three hundred years:

30 September 1648. About this year, my dear and only sister, the Lady Danby, drew near her time for delivery of her sixteenth child. Ten whereof had been baptized, the other six were still-born ... After exceeding sore travail she was delivered of a goodly son ... she was exceedingly troubled with pains, so that she was deprived of the benefit of sleep for fourteen days, except a few frightful slumbers; neither could she eat ... and as she grew weaker ... giving a little breathing sigh, delivered up her soul. Although she was married to a good estate, yet did she enjoy not much comfort and I know she received her change with much satisfaction.

Mrs Thornton herself did not fare much better. Seven weeks after her marriage she was pregnant but the child was still-born, and afterwards she 'fell into a most terrible shaking ague ... the hair on my head came off, my nails of my fingers and toes came off, my teeth did shake, and ready to come out and grew black.' Then she bore three children in three years. With the fifth, 'I was on the rack in bearing my child with such exquisite torments as if each limb were divided from the others ... but the child almost strangled in the birth, only living about half an hour.' Three years later her sixth child was born and died, then came the seventh, accompanied 'by a most violent and terrible flux of blood ... that my dear husband and children and friends had taken their last farewell'. She survived, though, to produce two more children 'after an exceeding sharp and perilous time' and both children died.

Madame de Sévigné, like so many mothers, endured the birth of her daughter and then had to watch that daughter give birth in her turn. She writes desperately to her son-in-law:

Do you imagine I gave her to you so that you might kill her, so that you might destroy her health, her beauty and her youth ... I don't come to find a woman who is pregnant and again pregnant and all the time pregnant.

And to her daughter:

If you get pregnant at this point, you may be sure that you will never get over it as long as you live. M. de Grignan is crowing too loud. If he succumbs to the temptation, don't believe he loves you. If M. de Grignan destroys [your beauty] you may take it as proven that his affection is not of sterling quality.

One hundred years later, Madame de Staël observed equally bitterly: 'The laws of morality seem to be suspended in the case of relations between men and women; a man passes off as good even though he may have inflicted great pain upon a fellow creature, so long as she is a woman.' To underline her feelings, the young Madame du Châtelet died in childbirth, which incident – according to the gossipy Sainte-Beuve – launched her impregnator, Saint-Lambert, in society.

All these women were in a comfortably-off minority – what of the poor majority? If a woman was married to a wealthy man, she could at least escape one of the worst ordeals of her poorer sisters – having a baby in hospital. Doctors wished to practise their trade and the Church wished to save souls, so the streets were regularly scoured for the poor, the diseased and the dying, sufferers from plague, malaria, typhoid, dysentery, venereal diseases and smallpox, all of whom were lumped together in the large hospital wards. And with them, often sharing the same beds, were women in labour. There, poked and probed by the hands of a doctor who knew nothing of infection and came straight from dissecting a putrescent corpse, they died of that scourge of childbirth for hundreds of years – childbed or puerperal fever. Sometimes entire wards of birthing women were decimated by this infection and though its cause was discovered by Ignaz Semmelweis in the nineteenth century, he was hounded into a lunatic asylum for daring to impugn the profession of medicine. As his contemporary, the historian Jules Michelet, observed: 'A woman is not only ill during fifteen or twenty days in every month, but she is for ever subjected to the eternal wounds of love ... this century will be known as the century of women's illnesses, of her despair and abandonment.' More than fifty years were to pass before the fever was brought under control and even as late as 1929 over 40 per cent of maternal deaths in the United States were due to this disease.

Even those women for whom sex was a business were forced to regard childbirth as an occupational hazard. I often think of Boswell's peregrinations through darkest London when the urge drove him to find a prostitute. He is torn between lust and the fear of contracting the pox. To this end (an apt phrase in this case) he armours himself in an iron device and moans bitterly that this often fails him and he is infected. He is honest and therefore likeable but I find his ruminations hard to read without wincing on behalf of those nameless shadows into whose flesh this awesome battering ram was pushed. And, if Boswell's device did not protect him from the pox, neither could it have protected them from pregnancy. Their penalty, and the child's too, is not pretty to contemplate.

Most of the great courtesans of the Italian Renaissance – and, quite likely, courtesans throughout history back to the hetaerae of Greece – were themselves the result of illicit love or lust. When they had children they tried to pass the infants off as their brothers' or sisters' offspring or the children of close relatives, to spare the child the slur of being a bastard. The daughters of courtesans were often only two years into their teens when they began to ply the only lucrative and independent trade they could and an unwanted pregnancy, inherently wretched, must have meant several penniless months.

The prostitute's other occupational hazard was venereal disease (which her clients would then pass on to their wives). In *Il Lamento della Cortigiana Ferrarese*, Beatrice describes her horrible encounter with syphilis, a disease that probably accounted for many young deaths. It reached epidemic proportions in Europe at the beginning of the sixteenth century and crippled Beatrice, reducing her to lower and lower brothels and ending her life in a hospital for venereal diseases.

Most of the children who were born of adultery or of prostitution at that time were either disposed of for good or farmed out to the country, where the odds on life were only slightly better. Love children they were sometimes called but they themselves saw little enough of love. True, among the gentry of the seventeenth century, bastards did better for themselves. Illegitimate and legitimate offspring were often brought up side by side as they had been in the Middle Ages, a form of polygamy for the women concerned, but considered natural enough by the men. Bastards, then, were even looked upon as slightly superior beings. Brantôme, who had served at the French courts of Charles IX and Henry III, wrote: 'These improvised children produced by stealth are far more gallant than those produced heavily, dully and at leisure,' and that was for a while the prevailing attitude. The writer Guillaume Bouchet believed that bastards were wittier than legitimate children because they had been conceived during ardent love-making when the seed of both parties was well mixed. But these were the fathers' bastards, the fathers made the rules and so they could afford to take an interest in their natural children. If you were a King, of course, like Louis XIV, you could be sure that every great noble in the land was happy to marry your many bastards. Shame and death were reserved for the bastards of noblewomen.

Ninon de Lenclos, the most famous free-love rebel of her time, sent her first illegitimate daughter away and then had to repel the advances of her illegitimate son, who did not know of the relationship. When she told him, the young man stabbed himself and died in his mother's arms, a seventeenth-century Oedipus. Other, less fortunate bastards died much earlier – Paris was littered with abandoned infants and the sixteenth-century preacher Olivier Maillard protested indignantly about the many babies thrown into latrines and rivers. Infanticide was always one of the most prevalent forerunners of contraception, practised by desperate women across time and the world. From 1861 to 1958, 431 women were sentenced to death in England and Wales; of the 391 reprieved, some 295 had killed their own children, as had one hundred of the 123 women reprieved from the death sentence between 1900 and 1949. In 1978, in Brazil, the number of abandoned children whose parents could not afford to bring them up was estimated at 15 million.

Rebecca Smith was hanged in 1849, the last woman to be executed in Britain for the murder of her infant child. She was forty-four, ill, undernourished, living in great poverty and almost illiterate. She had borne eleven children to her husband Philip Smith and she confessed that though four had died of various diseases, she had killed the other seven. Her husband was a drunkard, seldom earned any money and Rebecca was forced to work all day in the fields before coming home to care for her family. She told the judge at her trial that she had murdered her children 'to prevent them from coming to want'. Neighbours described Mrs Smith as a very pious woman who attended services regularly.

Those anguished mothers who did not kill their children paid to have them 'adopted' and the industry of baby-farming grew, another comment on the fact that being female did not automatically confer maternal feelings. Margaret Waters was one of eight women baby-farmers hanged for the murder of the children in their care between 1870 and 1907 and she herself may have accounted for as many as thirty-five infants, all the pathetic 'love-children' of women betrayed. When the police were finally called to Margaret Waters's home they found eleven emaciated babies, drugged, sick, covered in sores – as the children died Mrs Waters and her sister would dispose of their shrivelled bodies on waste land.

If the mothers of these children had feared social ostracism less or been able to obtain abortions, the children would have been spared their suffering, though the mothers might have paid with their lives. Abortion, or the attempt at it, is the last heavy penalty that women have paid for love throughout history, and we can only guess at the deaths and permanent injuries it has caused. I do not think it exaggerated to guess that from the dawn of patriarchy – that is to say, from the time when women ceased to be able to control men's access to their bodies – right up to today, few fertile women with several children have not at least once in their child-bearing lives attempted, however half-heartedly, either to abort themselves or procure an abortion. Yvette Guilbert wails of men in her memoirs of the 1890s, '. . . and love . . . their way of making and unmaking it, the abandonments, the miseries, the abortions . . .' and her wail echoes down the centuries.

One last tribulation that women have had to bear for love of individual men all through the ages is the knowledge, however shadowy and suppressed, that men as a whole believed the female sex at best inferior to them and at worst vessels of every iniquity, to be held in contempt, to be disliked, hated or feared and, saddest blow of all, to be regarded, often, as creatures whose very love could in some way emasculate, weaken or even doom a man to eternal damnation. St Augustine, two thousand years ago, believed that women's charms would imperil his chances for heaven; today's footballers believe the same charms will put paid to their chances of winning a match. Women, risking their lives, fell in love; men, risking nothing but some chimera they had invented themselves, held them at arm's length while they indulged in a spiritual struggle, succumbed to the woman's infernal powers and blamed, afterwards, the hapless loving creature for her evil ways. The wretched Héloïse, madly in love with Abélard, was deliberately seduced by him and when her cruelly medieval uncle had him castrated, was forced by her lover to enter a convent as punishment. Still loving, she wrote asking him if he had ever loved her and he answered, spitefully, 'My love was but concupiscence and did not deserve the name of love. I spent all my miserable passion upon you.' Nina Epton calls Héloïse 'a great saint of love', but how different was her love and her fate from many other lesser-known women?

J. K. Stephen, Cambridge don and tutor to the Prince of Wales, wrote some doggerel on the subject in 1883:

> If all the harm that women have done
> Were put in a bundle and rolled into one

Earth would not hold it
The sky could not enfold it
It could not be lighted or warmed by the sun
Such masses of evil
Would puzzle the devil
And keep him in fuel while Time's wheels run.

And in 1930 Julian Bell, also at Cambridge, described the female students as 'bottled snakes', a phrase most thriftily stuffed with venom. But it was par for the course and doubtless one of those bottled snakes doted upon him at the time. And it is in our own time that the classic pornographic description of what men expect from a woman in love and how they feel about that love was written. *The Story of 'O'*, published pseudonymously, tells of an anonymous woman, everywoman, in love with a man named René. He persuades her that if she really loves him, she will do whatever he commands and a sexual torture chamber is what he commands, with himself and other men of his choice as torturers. 'O' is whipped, repeatedly raped, branded, buggered and her body in every other way abused. She is handed by René to his friends for their delectation and as proof of her love for him. She is humiliated, burned, kept half-naked, chained, treated far worse than any animal, all in the name of love.

'You are here to serve your masters,' proclaims the credo of René, her lover, and his friends:

'Your hands are not your own, nor are your breasts, nor, most especially, any of your body orifices, which we may explore or penetrate at will. You have lost all right to privacy or concealment. Both this flogging and the chain are intended less to make you suffer, scream or shed tears than to make you feel, through this suffering, that you are not free but fettered, and to teach you that you are totally dedicated to something outside yourself. When you leave here, you will be wearing on your third finger an iron ring, which will identify you. By then you will have learned to obey those who wear the same insignia.'

There is much more in the same vein, details of the daily floggings 'O' will endure and the daily abuses she will accept as part of her lover's requirements. Through them all, 'O' loves René. Through all the most hideous torments she is asked – and gladly hastens – to say 'I love you' over and over and over again. Love is the only thing that matters at all, after all. And Maurice Girodias the publisher of '*O*', swears the author is a woman.

But, in spite of the horrors lying in wait for them round every corner, the constant threat of death and torture, disinheritance and poverty, shame, exile, crippling disease, endless pregnancies, pain, the fearful risks of abortion, hellfire and damnation, the agonies of losing children and losing the lovers who were their only salvation, women continued to risk everything for a kind of loving and many of them did it impudently, recklessly and with a high courage. The Aphrodites of the eighteenth century, for instance, were the lady members of an exclusive and scandalous club, immensely expensive to join and frequented only by the social élite. In a house near Montmorency adorned with statues of the gods and goddesses of love and screened from prying eyes by woods and mazes and pavilions, the ladies met and bedded the gentlemen of their choice. One indefatigable Aphrodite confided to her journal that during twenty years she had had 4,959 amorous rendezvous that included princes and prelates, officers and rabbis, tycoons and noblemen, commoners, valets, musicians, Negroes, two uncles, twelve cousins and 1,614 foreigners of mixed backgrounds. A swinger indeed and an intrepid one, willing to outface every hazard that confronts a woman when she makes love or lust. Madame, I curtsy to you in deepest admiration.

FOUR

The Ethics

'Whatever you do, I'll love you true.'

Perhaps the very fact that love took so much courage, exacted so high a toll from women, explains the other outstanding fact about women and love – our blanket acceptance of everything about it and lemming-like blindness to any disagreeable or disturbing feature in the beloved. In order to keep what we gambled so much to get we become arrant cowards. On that love altar we sacrifice even the most basic of human principles. Nothing, it appears, has been too great, too valuable, too sacred, too deeply believed to jettison. We have wilfully ignored the most primitive of decencies, we have condoned the most horrific of crimes and, like Abraham, we have frequently laid out our own children on the sacrificial rock at the Great God Love's command.

Women have children as part of their love-centred existence and this, more than anything else, defines them in their love-roles. At the core of maternal love is the idea that this, out of all other relationships on earth, is the one that cannot be broken, the true marriage vow, till death do us part. My child, goes the unwritten law, right or wrong. Psychopath, rapist, thug or pimp, I your mother will always love you. Flesh of my flesh for ever, I will cherish you through evil and love you to the hangman's noose and beyond: I shall adore you when the world abhors you, I shall be your companion across the Styx and your light in the underworld below.

Thus is created the image of perfect love that springs from the womb and the infant therein and metamorphoses into the loving woman/mother with her son/man. And society cherishes this image because the recipients of such all-embracing devotion are mostly men and society's mores are set by men. Fathers are not outstanding for their uncritical love of their children, husbands are in no way tied by custom to such total loyalty to wives. The concept of devotion unto death was manufactured as a kind of last-ditch placebo for the doers of this world, the masculine sex.

Obviously, women are a ready target for this propaganda, whatever ethical detachment they might have had already breached by the most intimate of human bonds. Once anyone – but women are the ones – has cradled and nursed an infant in its infinite vulnerability, complete helplessness and innocence, it becomes more difficult to harden the heart, to refuse to see – through the oafish adult body and the grainy pitted skin – the little child that once was, hair curling soft as down on the tissue-thin fontanelle. But a man, an adult, is not a child, he has swallowed the child and absorbed it into his adult frame. And if the man is evil the woman who loves him has a fearful responsibility to herself and to her society to recognize that evil, even though society will certainly sanction and often admire her for refusing to do so.

Behind every great man is a woman, we say, but behind every monster there is a woman too, behind each of those countless men who stood astride their narrow worlds and crushed other human beings, causing them hideous suffering and pain. There she is in the shadows, a vague female silhouette, tenderly wiping blood from their hands, scraping splintered bones from their boots. Nothing could make clearer the position of women as body servants and slaves because only slaves are, quite literally, *not* paid to ask questions and pass judgments. Absolute unquestioning loyalty is expected more of those we do not pay than of those we do, often, perhaps, because unconsciously we confuse non-payment with no payment required. Mother did it for nothing, loved me for nothing, stood by me for nothing. Wife is not paid either, therefore she must love me in the same way. Free services are quickly equated with the idea that those services are given from the fullness of a heart, and the guilt of non-payment is easily banished from the top of the mind. The fury of the slave owner, deceived, always amazed me until I realized that the boss deceived himself. I do not pay, therefore this must be done out of love because what was once done out of love was not paid. It is a terrible confusion and has cost many a slave's life.

That is the case, however slender, for the monster and his view of love. The motives of the woman behind him are less forgivable because lacking the excuse of monstrosity, yet people who love and service a monster are in some way monstrous themselves and bear some of the responsibility for the monster's deeds. It is, indeed, one of the more outrageous tenets of society that there is something not only forgivable but positively admirable about such lovers. The most generous interpretation is that all of us recognize our own propensity to evil – there but for the grace of God go I – and, shivering ever so slightly at the thought, hope that whatever we do *someone* will continue to love us. The worst interpretation is, I fear, the truth. To love is not counted among the earnestly acquired virtues of any moral code but put down to a pure and uncontrollable emotion. We cannot believe, as we wish to believe, that love must soar to the greatest heights of sacrifice unless we incorporate its twisted Janus face, a love that perseveres through the loved one's utmost cruelties and degradations, without censure.

Eva Braun, Hitler's mistress, who lived with him and, we suppose, loved him throughout his hellish reign until they died together in a dank bunker, remains in our memories as a very ordinary, prettyish woman of little consequence, slightly plump in her one-piece swimming costume, waving from balconies, romping genteelly at Berchtesgaden, an overgrown schoolgirl with floppy brown hair no more to be associated with Hitler's fearful deeds than a pet dog. But such women are, indeed, pet dogs, unaware of the grisly work done during the day by the masters who caress them at night and if reluctantly made aware, too staunch, too steadfast in love's name to blame or judge. Women must be havens, safe and calm harbours where the butcher can lay down his axe and the killer his head. Do not ask for whom the bell tolls because you might be informed that it tolls for your lover's victim. Poor Eva, we think, if we think at all. Yet we must know that such women have deliberately blinded and deafened themselves to the agony of anyone but their lovers. That marks them as accomplice psychopaths.

Franz Stangl was an ordinary Austrian cop when he met and married Teresa, his wife. He loved her and she loved him and they continued to love each other for thirty-five years until they were parted by his death. A-a-h. How romantic. Mind you, Teresa Stangl admits she was terribly angry when her husband volunteered to join the Austrian Nazi Party:

I just knew that day that he wasn't telling me the truth. And the thought that he had lied to me all this time, he whom I had believed incapable of lying, was terrible for me. And to think – oh, it was a terrible blow, just a terrible blow. My man . . . a Nazi . . . It was our first real conflict – more than a fight. It went deep. I couldn't . . you know . . . be near him, for weeks, and we had always been so close; this had always been so important between us. Life became very difficult.

But not, of course, *too* difficult – love surmounts such obstacles, this is what love is for. Frau Stangl, a devout Catholic herself, managed to surmount the next obstacle, too, though with misgivings. Franz signed the Party's form renouncing his allegiance to the Catholic Church. 'That was the second awful blow for me: finally we couldn't talk about it any more.'

To test her love further, Franz Stangl was sent as police superintendent to a pleasant, well-to-do suburb of Berlin, to the General Foundation for Institutional Care. There he was told his future duties. He reported to Schloss Hartheim, pleased still to be in Austria and close to his beloved wife. His duties were to supervise the gassing of 'patients' – the first stage of Hitler's euthanasia programme. For years, while countless thousands of 'patients' were killed at Hartheim, Franz Stangl saw his wife frequently. She asked what he was doing but only casually, since she was used to her Franz being unable to discuss service matters. Frau Stangl was, on her own admission, aware of the existence of the euthanasia programme, but says she did not know Schloss Hartheim 'was one of those places' till after the war.

Franz Stangl's second promotion made him Kommandant of Sobibor. 'I can't describe to you what it was like,' said

Stangl to Gitta Sereny who interviewed him in prison after the war:

The smell. Oh God, the smell. It was everywhere. Wirth wasn't in his office. I remember, they took me to him . . . he was standing on a hill, next to the pits . . . the pits . . . they were full . . . full . . . I can't tell you; not hundreds, thousands, thousands of corpses . . . oh God. That's where Wirth told me – he said that was what Sobibor was for. And that he was putting me officially in charge.

Now Frau Stangl was married to a man whose work was supervising the mass murder of a race, a promotion from merely gassing those considered 'unworthy to live', the criminally insane, the mentally deficient, the tubercular and, of course, the odd gipsy, homosexual and political hostage. Under Stangl, about 100,000 men, women and children were gassed. Herr Stangl ordered specially tailored riding-boots and white jodhpurs and jacket. Staying at a nearby house on one of her visits to her husband, Frau Stangl was told by a drunken officer exactly what was happening at Sobibor. She was horrified.

When he rode up and saw me from afar, his face lit up – I could see it. It always did – his face always showed his joy the moment he saw me. He jumped off his horse and stepped over – I suppose to put his arm round me. But then he saw at once how distraught I was. 'What's happened?' he asked. 'The children?' I said, 'I know what you are doing in Sobibor. My God how can they? What are *you* doing in this? What is your part in it?'

Franz Stangl eventually calmed his wife, telling her he was only in charge of construction work. She says she cried and sobbed and couldn't bear him to touch her.

He just kept stroking me softly and trying to calm me. Even so, it was several days before I . . . let him again. I can't quite remember the sequence of events, but I know I wouldn't have parted from him in anger.

Not long afterwards came the final promotion. Herr Stangl was made Kommandant of Treblinka, the largest of the five death camps in a two-hundred-mile circle around Warsaw. He described his arrival there:

I drove there, with an SS driver. We could smell it kilometres away. When we were about fifteen, twenty minutes' drive from Treblinka, we began to see corpses by the [railway] line, first just two or three, then more, and as we drove into Treblinka station, there were what looked like hundreds of them – just lying there – they'd obviously been there for days, in the heat. In the station was a train full of Jews, some dead, some still alive. Treblinka that day was the most awful thing I saw during all of the Third Reich, it was Dante's Inferno. It was Dante come to life. When I entered the camp and got out of the car on the square I stepped knee-deep into money: I didn't know which way to turn, where to go. I waded in notes, currency, precious stones, jewellery, clothes. They were everywhere, strewn all over the square. The smell was indescribable: the hundreds, no, thousands of bodies everywhere, decomposing, putrefying. Across the square, in the woods, just a few hundred yards away on the other side of the barbed-wire fence and all around the perimeter of the camp, there were tents and open fires with groups of Ukrainian guards and girls – whores, I found out later, from all over the countryside – weaving drunk, dancing, singing, playing music.

But efficient Stangl took over, cleared up the mess, planted flowers on the station banks and began to welcome the transport trains from Warsaw. Five or six thousand Jews were gassed daily before lunch under his aegis, then he ate his meal and had a little nap. There he ruled, there men were hanged upside-down, there dogs were trained to attack the genitals. The official figure given for deaths Stangl supervised is 900,000. A Polish underground worker, station supervisor at Treblinka from the day the death camp went into action to the day it was razed, counted every truck that passed, the figures of its contents written clearly on its sides by the ever-efficient Germans.

'I have added them up over and over and over,' he says. 'The number of people killed at Treblinka was 1,200,000 and there is no doubt about it whatever.'

And what of the loving wife during this time, the wife married to the man named in an official commendation as 'the best camp commander in Poland'? Why, she was busy with women's work. On one of his brief visits to her 'we started our youngest, Isolde'.

Can we excuse Frau Stangl, say she was a victim of events she never understood, believe she was bewildered and confused, afraid for her children, caught up in the general chaos of the holocaust? Surely we can say, at the very least, what could she have done? How could she, a mere woman and loving wife, possibly have attempted to change the inevitable?

Gitta Sereny put a question to her after her husband's death in 1971:

Would you tell me what you think would have happened if at any time you had faced your husband with an absolute choice; if you had said to him: 'Here it is; I know it's terribly dangerous, but either you get out of this terrible thing, or else the children and I will leave you.' If you had confronted him with these alternatives, which do you think he would have chosen?

Frau Stangl took more than an hour to answer that question. She lay on her bed and she cried and then she composed herself and answered:

I have thought very hard. I know what you want to know. I know what I am doing when I answer your question. I am answering it because I think I owe it to you, to others, to myself; I believe that if I had ever confronted Paul [her pet name for Stangl] with the alternatives: Treblinka or me; he would – yes, he would, in the final analysis, have chosen me.

Teresa Stangl, a small pretty woman from Linz, could have persuaded one of the nine camp commandants of Nazi Germany to leave his post and flee. It is impossible to tell what repercussions this might have had, how many others might have been given a flash of humanity, a burgeoning resistance, through this event. But though she loved her husband deeply – *because* she loved her husband deeply – she did nothing. No one had ever suggested to her that love has some morality, that to be 'in love' did not excuse horror outside the cosy family circle, that responsibility to the outer world must intrude. Blinkered, devoted, worried but faithful, whenever she had the opportunity she received her man into her bed, fresh from the naked shit-stained Jews, clutching their babies, whipped into the chambers. And in so doing, she lived out to the extreme the article of our faith: love conquers all.

The view that women are the natural guardians of

morality is not my view. In essence, women have the same proclivities as men towards good or evil. Nevertheless a large part of the female sex has been forced into the guardian role through history, if only because the strictures of society have weighed more heavily upon them and their opportunities for action have been very much more limited. Confined, in both senses, their habitat has always been love or what passed for love, an intimacy with the personal feelings of those around them, husbands, sons and lovers. So women are the mirrors that best reflect the intrinsic amorality of love – the record of men loving or living with monsters is thin as women monsters are thin; powerless, bounded by domesticity, it is hard to wreak much havoc in the world.

Women like Eva Braun and Teresa Stangl – and all the women behind the brutes of history from Caligula to the Marquis de Sade, from Herod to Stalin to Idi Amin – were intimate with men whose decisions were responsible for widespread massacres and innumerable crimes against humanity, other women and other women's children, too. But the women are also legion who have loved, protected or resigned themselves to cruel mini-autocrats within the family circle. That they have had excuse is obvious: fear and total dependency do not make it easy to rebel, but courage must always contend with expediency and face apparently hopeless obstacles – what is courage, otherwise? And there are many women who have lacked this courage even in defence of their children, weakened perhaps by their powerlessness but weakened far more by the insistent ethic: 'To have and to hold from this day forward, *for better for worse* . . . to love and to cherish till death us do part.'

A woman I know would tell you she loves her son dearly and abhors any form of corporal punishment. Her husband, a man with a violent temper, regularly beats him. Each time she shivers upstairs until the beating is over and then dispenses comfort to both – the son for his injuries, the husband for his repentant tears. It is a pathetic role and in many ways repellent but she acts in this way with no misgivings because it is approved. She is a Florence Nightingale, an innocent amid the strife, her soul pure, her conscience clear, distraught but blameless, a ministering angel. It does not occur to her that action to stop what she considers wrong is any part of her duty. Oh, of course she implores mitigation on behalf of her son, of course she does her best to plead his case. Countless examples have certainly taught her the uselessness of such pleading – the temper flares, the belt descends as remorselessly as ever – but she dares do no more, she says. She is, in fact, a coward. Or worse, perhaps she unconsciously relishes what she sees as continual evidence that she is so much better than her husband and so very indispensable to her son. Compassion, in the world that judges women, is a virtue of the highest order and who would condemn her for a constant flow of pity towards both males? But pity is a poor and passive thing, last resort of the impotent. Better by far if this woman exercised pity with its proper corollaries – righteous anger and remedial action. Stroking the brow of the wronged is what you do when you can do nothing more and all women can do something more, though they may risk everything. But that is what courage is about.

When accused, this woman says, her blue eyes wide: but I love him. I pity him. He cannot help it. He is so *sorry*, afterwards. Thus she deceives and connives in the corruption of her loved ones; adored by both as saintly, she eats away at their resolve, soothing the terror of her son, forgiving the rage of her husband. And, of course, betraying without a second's thought her principle that corporal punishment is wrong, wrong in all circumstances and by whomsoever administered. What course of action could she take that would be in any way effective, have any bearing on stopping this abuse? Quite possibly, none. But you do not stand by your principles only when you think your stance will be effective. Such outcomes cannot be judged beforehand and, anyway, should not rule out action. A woman must do what a woman must do: period. Use what little power she may have, announce her instant departure, with son, if the husband attacks him once more, and follow it through. Only thus is she beginning to show true love, for her husband, for her son and for her principles. Love, in such cases, must be made of sterner stuff than a cool hand on a repentant brow. Those who act as victims are victims, deserve to be. Those who are bruised and battered for their beliefs are no victims. If the only weapon against injustice is disassociation, physical and mental, then that weapon, at least, must be used.

The mother's betrayal of her children to the abuse of her husband is a constant theme and a very shameful one. It is no accident that those children grow up hating the violent father and hating, too, the cringing mother. Quite likely, the hatred of that mother is far more damaging to them since it is oblique, twisted, often apparently inexplicable, always charged with ambivalence, the fear that one is hating the wrong person in the wrong way. Hating a physically violent man is straightforward in comparison and probably less damaging. Surveys of battered sons show that they too grow up to be battering husbands. The phenomenon is put down to the climate of violence in which the boy has grown up, to which he has not only become accustomed but grown to see as the only way to live. I think it is equally well explained as an adult revenge against the creep, his mother, who gave lip-service to love, who pretended to be his protector and yet who allowed his assault to continue, daily, without proper action. In his heart of hearts he perceives women as frauds and hypocrites, covering wounds with soft words. Powerful adults who, when tested, dissolve into jelly. Never to be trusted.

Dory Previn, singer, writer of lyrics, composer, was imprisoned with her mother and her new sister in one room for four and a half months by her mad father. Somehow, she endured it at the time and paid for that quiet endurance years later with repeated mental breakdowns. When first I read about it, it seemed one of those natural catastrophes that occasionally beset children – the father was mad, he did not know what he was doing and against madness there is no defence and no blame. But when the facts are set out, they acquire a much more horrific dimension – her mother could have avoided the damage to her powerless child, action was available to her, she was not the pure victim of circumstance:

Actually we could have gotten out any time. There was a door. The one that swung open into the kitchen. I was too small to stick up for my rights. But if Mama wanted to, she could have just taken us two kids and walked out of that rotten room. But she didn't . . .

> from then on
> we were a family
> we even had some fun
> the boards
> on the dining-room door
> came down
> and daddy put away his gun and
> I forgot it happened
> like something
> i'd been dreaming
> till eighteen odd years later
> when i suddenly woke up
> screaming

Many children know that sense of betrayal that turns, in later life, to a consuming and useless anger against the mother. The mother who could have done something and did nothing. The mother who said she was doing nothing for our sakes and was doing nothing for her own, for love. Dory Previn's mother took her away to her grandparents, away from her mad father who beat the mother up, but she brought her back because the Catholic Church said this was her man and for other, more personal reasons not shared by Dory.

We were home in less than a week. Then it started. All that pleading and begging. All that sobbing and stuff. Down on his knees. All those promises. Broken. Hers. Not his. He never promised to take me to see the freaks in Barnum and Bailey's. He never promised me chicken croquettes and a terrific experience inside of Liberty's head. He never said I could stay and listen to Grandpa Shannon's watch till the day I died. He never promised we wouldn't have to go back there. Her promises didn't mean anything. I finally understood that.

In her betrayal, the mother teaches her daughters to endure and not to act, as she has endured and not acted. Conditions her daughters to be victims, as she is a victim, as if being a victim was a career.

'How about if I stood up to him, Mama? Maybe he'd back down and we could get out. He wouldn't back down to the pope on a bike. What if I answered him back and took my chances of getting hit in the mouth?'

And then the cunningest appeal of all is brought into the open:

'He wouldn't hit you, Dorothy! I'm the main one to him! If you cross him he'll kill *me*! And if I die, *you'll* be responsible.' I was certainly scared of his insane temper, all right. But I almost hated her. Forgive me, God, but she had me hog-tied with her trepidations. If it was just me that would have got whacked, I'd have done it. In fact, I think I'd have enjoyed it, if such a thing is possible. At least then, I'd have gotten it off my chest. And I wouldn't have to bite the sheets every night after I said my prayers. But if he killed her because I took the bull by the horns. God-in-Heaven, a child couldn't be responsible for her own mother's death, could she? So he went on yelling. And she went on screaming. And I sat quiet.

There is nothing out of the way about Dory Previn's story. Anyone whose father is an autocrat, by virtue of no opposition, and whose mother is a victim, by virtue of no guts, has lived through the same scenario. Miss Previn endured more drama than most because her father was insane and not just an autocrat, but perhaps his insanity spread because it was given no boundaries? What is the use of a mother's day-to-day sacrifices for her children if, in every important way, she betrays them, forces them to undergo horrors for the sake of her love, her needs, teaches them the inevitability of the bully-boy's triumph? Day after day in a hundred million homes, children watch as the father violates the mother's beliefs, watch as she does nothing, says nothing. The spark of resistance in them is crushed, the awful strength of the weak indoctrinates them. Mother and father play out the roles assigned to them, roles they fearfully enjoy, and the children are deformed for life by the fall-out. Society helps them not at all. The judgment passed on their father: of course he should not do those things (but men will be men). The judgment on their mother: poor thing, what could she do and she so saintly, keeping the family together, sticking to her husband through thick and thin. Society proffers him no reward for better behaviour, more control. Society allows no stiffener for her backbone, no ethic for rebellion, no praise for a refusal to countenance abuse.

Here and there, you may read stories in newspapers. A man has raped two young girls. A man has sexually assaulted and then killed a child. The police believe he is being sheltered by a woman who knows what he has done or, at the very least, suspects. Do they threaten, do they command, this woman to give up the man? Do they cite the fact of her crime under the law, list the penalties for her sheltering? Rather, they implore, they plead, they appeal to her sense of duty, but they falter as they plead. After all, what she is doing is only the extreme of what men expect women to do in general. Protect no matter what, shelter no matter what. When the man is found, no charges are pressed against the woman because, like a faithful dog, she was only doing what society expects her to do. A social conscience in a woman is not nice, it is a violation of her role. If, occasionally, the woman does come forward and give information about her man, gooseflesh is raised upon society's skin. Though he has taken a child, tortured it, raped it, strangled it and buried it, she is still considered a quisling, treacherous, though no one may put it into words. Though she cling to him, defend him, refuse to condemn him, refuse to think of what he has done and to whom he has caused lifelong misery, she is found innocent. Her behaviour is considered natural, even praiseworthy, though we may not praise aloud.

The story of Charlie Manson and his adoring women followers is a graphic and hideous illustration of the kind of female passivity that colluded with his male mania for power to produce, between them, a monster capable of organizing the brutal slaying of eight people. In the name of love for Charlie, whom they turned into a god, a neo-Jesus, these girls allowed him to take complete control of their lives and, through them, the lives of others. For Charlie, they became zombies who offered themselves to any man he commanded, who hustled for him, served him and willingly subjected themselves to any and every degradation for him. For Charlie, they eventually slaughtered and, on trial for their lives, remained loyal to him. Outside the courtroom, other girls shrieked abuse at the prosecuting lawyers and tried to convert passers-by to Charlie's way of thinking. Two of these women had themselves given birth and yet nothing in this experience, no belief, no ethic, no milk of ordinary human kindness, prevented them delivering themselves over wholly to a bloodbath ordered by the beloved.

Vincent Bugliosi, the prosecuting lawyer said:

They seemed to radiate inner contentment. I'd seen others like this – true believers, religious fanatics – yet I was both shocked and impressed. Nothing seemed to faze them. They smiled almost continuously, no matter what was said. For them all the questions had been answered. There was no need to search any more, because they had found the truth. And their truth was 'Charlie is love'.

And if Charlie is love, then for Charlie's sake all horrors are justified, all sins made pure.

There is another sin that women commit in the name of love that has none of the drama of monsters condoned but may, in its own low-key way, have contributed to the prolonged immaturity of homo sapiens. I imagine all women have sinned in this way – I have, repeatedly – because we are given to believe that the sin is a virtue and a deeply feminine duty for which we are uniquely gifted. What we do, like heroines in old Hollywood movies, is to fling ourselves as living barriers between the deeds of our men and our children and the consequences of those deeds, arms stretched out to protect them, nobility staining every lineament. Thus we help to create what perhaps, in an access of motherhood, we actually want – permanent children. We constantly get in the way of and interfere with one of the greatest of life's teaching machines: as ye sow, so shall ye reap, and we do it principally on behalf of men. There we are, big fat cushions, safety nets to catch the highwire artistes who are only up there fooling around because we will not let them glimpse the abyss below. Fall on me, we shout, bouncing up and down invitingly, I'll look after you. I won't let you feel the shock that lies beneath. And so the men go on doing ludicrous and irresponsible things because we shield them from the full consequences of their actions. Well, otherwise, how would they know that we were important, essential, the pivot of their lives?

We have done our darndest, whenever we could, to distort the straightforward process that all living creatures need to learn for their best interests – if I do A, then B will result, this is the cause and that is the effect. Then we say, lovingly, 'Men are only grown-up boys, pretty ladies are their toys,' and the men smirk back at us fondly, never realizing that in our wisdom we have kept them from growing, kept them little court dwarfs for our toys, Jacks in a box. Love is the only thing that matters at all, after all.

FIVE

The Process

'You made me love you, I didn't want to do it.'

Once, when I was in Trinidad, I went to see a witch, or rather a wizard, an old black man with the pale eyes of the tropics. He was much visited by the younger island women because he made up and sold love potions. He showed me one plant out of which he brewed a substance which, if buried on a pathway regularly taken by the beloved, would induce him or her immediately to fall in love with his client. He also gave me the fleshy leaf of a kind of cactus. On this leaf I was instructed to scratch with my nail the name of my lover and then to put it away for a month between the pages of a heavy book. The point of this exercise was to find out if my lover was true to me. I did this, made half-credulous by an alien place and anxiety over my lover, an anxiety that easily overcomes most Western disbelief. When I looked at the leaf in a month's time, there along the edges were tiny buds, baby offspring that the wizard had said would be the sign that love was true. I was delighted, it was magical, I giggled and poked fun at it with friends but I have it still – and my lover too, for that matter.

Which is only to say that human beings, whether they live in London, New York or Trinidad, manage quite successfully to keep two contradictory ideas about love in their heads and believe both. The first is that love is beyond all human control, a bolt of lightning that strikes from mysterious heights and performs strange alchemies at random, and the other, its opposite, that love is open to mechanical manipulation, so that by doing certain things and being in certain places, an individual can force love to descend, can magic it up. Like those who believe that by standing in a pentagram and going through certain rituals, the powers of darkness, anarchy itself, can be tamed at least enough to bow to those rituals and appear; so lovers through the ages have been sure that the arbitrary and powerful love gods and goddesses can nevertheless be forced, through a potion, a plant, a series of actions, to do the helpless human's bidding and conjure love where love was not.

With every year of increasing knowledge about the human psyche and behaviour, the idea that love descends irrationally, without the slightest rhyme or reason, fades, though we may choose not to know it. It becomes clear that to a great extent we can control and manipulate this apparently uncontrollable emotion and where we cannot do so, there is growing evidence that the obstacle is only a lack of soon-to-be-available knowledge. A computer may be well or badly programmed but its potential is infinite – its current performance is only limited by what is known to those who feed it information. Where there are unfathomable mysteries, there will be superstitious explanations. Gods will be invoked, spirits raised, rituals carried out in a blind attempt to ape cause and effect. As knowledge comes and reliable explanations are found for what seemed magical, the gods atrophy, the spirits die, the rituals are abandoned. Where control is possible – if I do A, B will always result – mysticism ceases. Human intelligence, however magical its expression, always assumes that things are ordered into cause and effect. When it doesn't know the cause, it pretends it does. So witch doctors guess that illness has some roots in the mind and try to manipulate the mind into cure and their reasoning only fails, if it fails, in mechanics and not in essence. There is of course a link between mind and body which Western knowledge has defined with psychiatry or mechanized with electric shocks and drugs rather than gesture and magic.

We already know something of the mechanics of love, the more primitive machinery by which we may control, invoke or exorcize it with some reliability. For generations men have looked upon it as a malady, a dis-ease and tried to find cures. The Arab philosopher Avicenna set down in the eleventh century seven ways in which love could be eased, altered and expelled. Savonarola, preaching in Florence in the 1490s, came up with nine, and there were many others whose aims and methods were summed up by Robert Burton in *The Anatomy of Melancholy,* published in 1621. Clearly, all these gentlemen were also aware that love had very little to do with anyone but the leisured and the rich because many of love's cures involved attempts to mimic poverty. Burton quotes in Latin, *'sine Cerere et Baccho friget Venus'* without Ceres and Bacchus (food and drink) Venus grows cold – and reasons that as an idle, sedentary life and liberal feeding are great causes of love, so labour, a slender and sparing diet, with continual busyness, are the best and most available means to prevent it. Ovid recommends: 'Love yields to business, be employed, you're safe,' and Guianerius advises the love sufferer that he should 'go with hair-cloth next his skin, to go bare-footed and bare-legged in cold weather, to whip himself now and then, as Monks do but, above all, to fast' – in other words, to copy as nearly as possible the life-styles of the majority of peasants. Because poor people 'fare coarsely, work hard, go wool-ward and bare', says Burton, *'non habet unde suum paupertas pascat amorem'*. Poverty lacks the means to feed love.

The ancients did not believe that absence made the heart grow fonder. Valerius Maximus urged that the lover 'as a sick man, must be cured by change of air' and the Roman poet Propertius added, 'My parents sent me to Athens; time and absence wear away pain and grief, as fire goes out for want of fuel.' Another cure much emphasized by Burton was a kind of seventeenth-century aversion therapy. Imagine your mistress as she will look when she grows old, he advises, knowing the sad fact that constant child-bearing made women old before their time. 'Those fair sparkling eyes will look dull, her soft coral lips will be pale, dry, cold, rough and blue, her skin rugged, that soft and tender superficies will be hard and harsh.' And he adds, 'That tyrant Time will turn Venus to Erinys; raging Time, care, rivels her upon a sudden; after she hath been married a small while ... she will be so much altered and wax out of favour, thou wilt not know her.'

And if all else fails, Burton quotes the advice of the

third-century Greek patriarch St John Chrysostom, a sobering exercise in reality:

When thou seest a fair and beautiful person, who would make your mouth water, a jolly girl and one you would find easy to love, a comely woman, having bright eyes, a merry countenance, a shining lustre in her look, a pleasant grace, wringing thy soul and increasing thy concupiscence; bethink thyself that it is but earth thou lovest, a mere excrement, which so vexeth thee, which thou so admirest and thy raging soul will be at rest. Take her skin from her face and thou shalt see all loathsomeness under it, that beauty is a superficial skin and bones, nerves and sinews; suppose her sick, now rivel'd, hoary-headed, hollow-cheeked, old: within she is full of filthy fleas, stinking, putrid, excremental stuff; snot and snivel in her nostrils, spittle in her mouth, water in her eyes, what filth in her brain.

And in case that didn't knock Eros for a Burton, he adds that the lover should examine his lady closely, in the light, when he will be sure to discover 'crooked nose, bad eyes, prominent veins, concavities about the eyes, wrinkles, pimples, red streaks, frechons, hairs, warts, neves, inequalities, roughness, scabredity, paleness, yellowness, frowns, gapes, squints'.

All these harangues reveal some most interesting beliefs (however unconscious) about love that are almost as prevalent today as they were in Burton's century. Love and poverty do not mix. Hard work, whether physical or mental, makes the growth of love unlikely and proves its irrelevance to the real interests of life. Men, who have choice in the matter, see love as an aberration and a distraction, something to be cured of rather than revelled in, and give it lip-service only in women. Men demand high standards of physical attraction in women before they contemplate love but apply none of those standards to themselves– they, apparently, never need to consider their own inner 'filth' or outward blemishes, whether warts, frowns or plain old age. Either they feel no blemishes can mar their essential desirability or they are blithely unaware of blemishes at all. Nothing could more clearly reveal the basic male tenets: men do not care to love but are innately lovable, women love but are not intrinsically lovable. And underlying this is an even more basic assumption, shattering in its tacit cynicism: love is the umbrella word for a simple dynamic between the sexes – women need men, no matter what kind of men, to survive, and men do not need women except for physical duties.

In many ways, the antidotes suggested by Burton and Co. are the forerunners of our twentieth-century aversion therapists, pedlars of out-of-love potions who manifest, by their methods or attempts at cure, their belief that love is a matter of the accidental juxtaposition of sensory inputs. Because these juxtapositions are random, we may substitute pieces of our own for the natural jigsaw: combining the swollen heart, not with roses and posies or moon and June, but with shocks and traumas and sickness to end love's pains. They operate the other side of the theory of fetishism, that sad and tiresome phenomenon whereby, it is believed, the child victim, caught by the sight of a passing foot, the hem of a fur coat, the ruffle of a feather boa, a covering of leather or the clammy envelope of his own rubber sheet, experiences at the same moment and purely by chance his first sexual upheaval and his poor brain, like a malfunctioning computer, fires two entangled neutrons with electric memory loads and never again manages to uncouple the fused tracks. He is doomed thereafter to time-consuming, expensive and embarrassing scenarios, for in order to gain access to one memory cell stored with sexual delight, he must accept its parasitic partner, the foot, the fur, the feather, the leather, the rubber. Or so we are told.

Fetishism and aversion therapy are both rather sad variations on the normal and general phenomenon of imprinting, which can be accurately pin-pointed in birds and some animals and happens more diffusely to children, too. At one time it was thought that behaviour of all kinds in all creatures fell into one of two categories: instinctive or learned. Nowadays, things have become a little more blurred because although there are clear examples of purely instinctive behaviour – a well-fed starling in an insectless cage will still make snapping motions at invisible flies in the air and many birds isolated from their species at birth will sing the species' song – a lot of what used to be thought learned behaviour is now believed to have a genetic admixture. Innate tendencies combine at certain times to trigger off learning processes that, if conditions are not right, cannot only be inhibited but actually impossible at any future time. It is as if the genes were little time bombs implanted in the child that go off at specific intervals, readying the brain to learn, say, language, and if the outside environment does not feed in language, the opportunity may be lost for ever.

Konrad Lorenz discovered that if he substituted himself early on for a mother duck, the ducklings 'imprinted' on him, the genetic code for love was triggered and from then on the ducklings regarded him as their parent. As yet we know much less about how this imprinting mechanism works in human beings but we know it does operate. It may account, for instance, for what we call 'love at first sight'. The child is imprinted with an image of another human being and responds ever after to similar human beings. Certainly, everyone who has talked to me about experiencing love at first sight mentions the accompanying feeling of intense familiarity. 'I felt I'd known him for ever,' said one girl. 'When I met Jean it was like meeting the Queen,' said a man, 'you know, you've seen so many photographs of her you feel she's one of the family.' As the song puts it, 'I know that we have met before and danced before, but who knows where or when.'

Though no one yet knows exactly when such imprinting occurs in the span of childhood, it is likely that the imprint is of the features and 'aura' of a close relative because the child will probably be surrounded by them most of the time. This rather confuses any analysis of love at first sight. Roughly, Freudians explain the phenomenon as a result of the Oedipus or Electra complex – the child, having repressed a first love for mother or father, glimpses something familiar later in an adult and promptly becomes infatuated, the nursery love reawakened and, this time, legitimate. Certainly, studies have shown a rather more than random resemblance between one or other parent and a chosen lover but this could as well be a result of imprinting as of any more abstract psychological explanation. The two theories obviously overlap. Even if we add, here, the Narcissus theory and believe that people fall in love with those who most resemble themselves (there are many husbands and wives who look at least as much alike as brothers and sisters), then all three theories overlap. No wonder animals practise incest as the easy way out.

All of my life, I have been attracted to men with an odd lifting of the upper lip, faintly resembling a sneer. My mother did not have this charming trait and neither did my father, but all my mother's brothers do. Am I supposed, then, to have an Uncle complex? I imagine so, since that upper lip is not a common feature. Yet my own experience heavily underlines the dangers inherent in this sort of 'imprinted' love – it is a childish attraction based on long-vanished needs. When I was eight years old, my uncles were my gods but they would not have suited me later, disguised as mates. That naturally did not stop me from falling once, twice or five times for that old upper lip and it took some fruitless years before I consciously put aside the imprinting and acknowledged that, for me, sneering upper lips were bad news, however initially sexy.

Of course, imprinting does not have to centre on a relative – if you come from that class in which nannies or maids cared for the children, your thing may be your nanny's face and good luck to you. There is a good 'nanny' example to be found among the birds: male zebra finches which had been reared by Bengalese finches were put with females of their own kind, with whom they mated – presumably because their genetic coding enabled them to 'recognize' their own. But the same male zebra finches were then given a choice of female zebra finches or female Bengalese finches and they all mated with their old 'nannies', the Bengalese finches. In other words, early imprinting appeared to be stronger even than the inherent leaning towards the same species. Obviously, if you get the two together as you most often do in animals as well as humans, when the genetic 'recognition' is combined with imprinting because those who care for you when young are also 'your own species', it is no wonder that so many of us fall for those who resemble ourselves, however little we may be conscious of it.

There is another trait which clearly triggers love and is also involved with inherent genetic coding – a childish appearance and the use of childish signals. The infant, animal or human, transmits these signals to release protective behaviour in mother and other adults. The young of many species have different-coloured coats or special markings, big heads in proportion to their bodies, relatively larger eyes, a chubby body shape and higher voices. All of us, as adults, make use of these innate releasing signals to arouse protectiveness in others. Dogs, when threatened, make themselves smaller and mew like puppies. Courting male birds flutter their wings like chicks and females beg for food in the same way. Male hamsters court females with cries like nestlings and the female roe deer in rutting attracts the buck with the same sounds used by kids to call their mother. When Walt Disney wants us to like an animal, it is drawn to look as much like a human baby as possible and it is no accident that the two great love goddesses of two generations, Marlene Dietrich and Marilyn Monroe, both have faces whose structure closely resembles children – large heads, big wide-apart eyes, small noses and soft blonde curls.

The flaw in this baby-love theory, until now, has been its inapplicability to the female. If childish signals in adults are thought to set off innate caring behaviour in other adults on the basis that such signals from a true infant are part of its survival mechanisms, geared to make the parents react, then surely it should be women, above all, who most strongly react to the same signals in adults. But is this so? What about the altogether adult, rugged and masculine types that women traditionally fall for – the Gary Coopers, Clark Gables, John Waynes, Oliver Reeds? My own view is that the infantile signals, given the dependent position of women until the present day, were ignored in men because they were overlaid by the woman's need for a father, for protection, and that the 'paternal' signals, meaning 'I will look after and fight for my woman and my children', were all-important.

Interestingly, the beginning of the women's liberation

movement and the subsequent increase in independence, financial and emotional, of women has marked a change in the kinds of men favoured by those women. The 'sugar daddy', who was quite often physically unattractive – ageing, fat, bald, short, ugly and anything but baby-like – is on his way out, his overlay of sexual signals (power, money, status, the paternal) made obsolescent by women's growing ability to provide these things for themselves and strengthened by the cult of youth which allows much younger men access to power and money. The stars of the new age are baby-faced to a much greater extent than ever before. Robert Redford, David Essex, the Osmonds, John Travolta – all have either quite obviously small features and a general air of appealing softness in their faces or, like Paul Newman and, say, Ryan O'Neal, a charm that contains heavy doses of boyishness and/or helplessness. Indeed, even the old, rugged stars and their equivalents in real life often combined 'protection' signals with what women naturally thought of as an endearing helplessness. What's more, many women were at pains to search out such infantile signals, almost as if they were intent on satisfying an inner urge for the 'baby' trigger. 'He may be husky but he can't boil an egg,' they say proudly of their superficially 'daddy' man and almost every woman, bar the very young, can produce tales, told with evident pleasure, of the bachelor squalor from which they rescued their man or the tide of dirty socks and fungoid dishes that accumulate around husbands in their absence. Most men use baby signals just as women do, when they need help. We all recognize the way men's voices go up by several notches when they are feeling under the weather, and illness itself is sometimes (some would say always) psychosomatic, a call for physical evidence of caring, a harking back to mother who might have been generally undemonstrative but turned up trumps when you took to your bed.

All these phenomena go on to a great extent below the level of consciousness and though many of us consciously use, for instance, the baby signalling, the manipulation involved is only, as it were, a turning up of the volume, since the message is already in the air or, rather, the genes. Women, particularly, are often accused of using a kind of fluffy helplessness manipulatively, the view being that underneath the flutter is a ruthlessly capable human being intent on her own ends. This may, in a sense, be true, but as women traditionally have had no other method of survival than the hope that a man or men would provide for them, it is hardly surprising that they soup up the infantile signals that have enabled all human beings to flourish under someone's wing. Using the weapons at hand is part of survival and only when women are given access to the male means of civilized living – job opportunities, equal pay, control over their reproduction and ways of caring for the results of reproduction that do not conflict with the first two needs – will this manipulation of an inherent pattern cease.

But we now know enough about the workings of the brain on at least a mechanistic level (that is, as a result of various experiments we know that certain things happen, though we don't, as yet, know why) and enough about psychiatry (including methods of making the brain yield up its secrets) to begin to be able to put together some broad formulae for the process of falling in love. No one has yet done this, mainly because the various disciplines, discoveries and techniques involved have been harnessed to more dubious ends. These ends have had to do mainly with the military, which creates an imperative lacking in love, but the information that has come out of the necessities of war is sufficient to show that its application to other forms of emotion would not be difficult, though in the wrong hands (and whose are the right hands?) almost as frightening. The techniques are as old as mankind but it has taken twentieth-century technology and knowledge to refine them to the point where their efficacy is pretty well guaranteed.

For hundreds of years, men, with their observational faculties sharpened by a desire for power over their fellow human beings, have noticed how certain conditions have led to fairly predictable kinds of behaviour and have set out to reproduce artificially what they observed to happen naturally or accidentally. The aim has been either to inspire within others a personal or ideological devotion – the two are often inextricably entwined – or to dislodge one set of beliefs, ideas or memories and replace it with another. The essence of the technique, shared down the ages by a wildly disparate army of power-seekers, is summarized in an experiment done some years ago on three litters of puppies.

One litter was consistently maltreated by their owner. The second litter was consistently well-treated and the third was alternately maltreated and well-treated. The result of this rather sad experiment was thus: the maltreated puppies grew into dogs that acted quite independently of their owner, as did the consistently well-treated dogs. But the on-again off-again puppies failed to make the transition, in adulthood, to independence and remained cringingly attached to their unpredictable master.

Within that one small experiment, practised on *canis domesticus*, are more of the rotten roots of unequal human love than most of us would care to contemplate. Within it we can also see a shadow of human emotional response from the religious inspiration of ancient faiths right through to the methodical brain-washing of modern warfare, not to mention the most basic example common to us all – the experience of the child vis-à-vis its parents.

A recent human equivalent of the puppy experiment concerns a group of American soldiers captured during the Korean war, who were physically abused, isolated, frightened and deprived of toilet facilities. Later, stinking with their own excrement, they were gently bathed and cleaned by other Koreans who continued to treat them gently and reassuringly. Most of them were then ready to accept as gospel whatever those Koreans wished to teach them. They were, in other words, brain-washed without the use of any more mechanistic technology than the experience of fear and self-disgust and the relief of that fear and self-disgust. The parallel with even the mildest memory of being a helpless child, with mother the unpredictable rescuer, is vivid.

Basically the same methods have been used through history and pre-history. Whatever was unpredictable, whether a catastrophe or a blessing, we invested with a worshipping ritual, as if something inherent in human beings believed that adoration, love, could assuage the worst excesses of the mystery. Our ancestors have worshipped, in one form or another, aspects of the weather and the seasons, animals, the stars, the dead, rivers, mountains, mythical monsters and even kinds of disease – all linked by a common bond, their existence as powers in themselves, uncontrollable by men, sometimes the source of happiness and well-being, sometimes deadly. There arose, naturally enough, individuals who served as intermediaries with these eccentric gods, who knew or learned the ways to heighten susceptibilities, who were able, in ritual, to condense the larger experience and create smaller waves of fear and disorientation, to be rewarded by some smaller benefit, mirroring hunger and the coming of the rain, fear and the fleeing of the animal, the death of the sun and its return. Because of their own mirror-rituals, they deflected some of the worship meant for the gods to themselves, so that they too were feared and therefore loved.

To a lesser extent, the same methods were used to make iron bonds of devotion within tribes and communities. The initiation rites used by ancient men upon their sons and those common in today's American universities, in Freemasonry or among the Hell's Angels show no real difference from each other. Isaac Schapera, Emeritus Professor of Anthropology at London University, describes one African tribe's initiation ceremony that seems typical of many: the boys are secluded for three months in a special camp, they are circumcised, they hunt game, run long distances at speed as a test of endurance, are occasionally subjected to starvation 'and many other rigorous forms of discomfort', and those who have been unruly or insolent in the past are whipped or punished by 'various ingenious forms of torture'. Meanwhile they are given instruction: 'The most important, known as the songs of the law, exhorted them to honour, obey and support the chief; to be ready to endure hardships and even death for the sake of the tribe; to be united as a regiment and to help each other.' American and German men may well recognize one or all of these practices as familiar.

Girls too, at the onset of menstruation, are sometimes excluded from the tribe for a year or more, in total isolation, visited once a day by another woman with food. Clearly, the underlying idea is to put death and rebirth into concrete form. To undergo this, the individual must be as disorientated and frightened as seems commensurate with the amount of love and loyalty demanded by the tribe.

As William Sargant points out in *The Mind Possessed* and *Battle for the Mind*, in different religions the same methods are used to attain quite different truths and the extensive literature of mysticism, with its instructions to the aspirant, confirms this.

Most significant of all is the initiation ceremony described by Ruth Benedict in *Patterns of Culture*, practised by those near-miraculously gentle people, the Zuñi tribe of Pueblo Indians of New Mexico:

Later, traditionally when the boy is about fourteen and old enough to be responsible, he is whipped again by even stronger masked gods . . . after the final whipping, the four tallest boys are made to stand face to face with the 'scare kachinas' [the punitive masked gods] who have whipped them. The priests lift the masks from their heads and place them upon the heads of the boys. It is the great revelation. The boys are terrified. The yucca whips are taken from the hands of the 'scare kachinas' and put in the hands of the boys who face them, now with masks upon their heads. They are commanded to whip the 'kachinas'. It is their first object lesson in the truth that they, as mortals, must exercise all the functions which the uninitiated ascribe to the supernaturals themselves.

Thus are the boys prepared to receive the secrets of their tribe and to keep them secret. Pain, terror, disorientation, yielding absolute loyalty and devotion.

The similarities between some of these examples of intense human emotion are striking. The whole of early childhood is a heightened emotional state and, later, such heights are also reached in initiations of various kinds, religious and political conversions, the prelude to brain-washing, spiritual possessions, drug experience, faith healing, seances and the traumas of war. In all these situations, the individual is faced with circumstances that are beyond his control because they are unpredictable, nervous excitation is extreme, the resulting exhaustion complete and the later 'rebirth' – the acceptance of beliefs hitherto either rejected or alien – unshakeable, inaccessible to reason. It is as if the earlier brain-grooves of memory and ideas were suddenly ironed out by intense electrical activity and new concepts imprinted in place of the old, unique in their strength and implacable aversion to facts.

To take an animal example: the famous Pavlovian dogs, carefully conditioned in behavioural reflexes, were trapped in their cages when the Neva river overflowed its banks in Leningrad in 1924. The water rose inexorably, the animals rose with it and were only rescued at the last minute when they were frantically keeping their noses above the flood. Some of the dogs were so terrified by their ordeal that they were dragged out in a state of total collapse. Pavlov found that these dogs, once recovered, had lost all memory of their conditioning and were, to all intents and purposes, untouched by his months of training. William Sargant, learning from this event, realized that in treating soldiers suffering from the horrible shocks of war the important thing was to create *any* sort of physical excitation in the brain, whether by drugs, electric shock treatment or in ways more closely related to the fearful memory. The method was not as important as the creation of excitation, which in itself would lead to the temporary collapse and revival, clean of the horrors. Priests, witch doctors, voodoo cultists, mediums, the military, great orators and preachers, exorcizers and many other people have known and practised much the same techniques for generations.

The growth of a certain kind of passionate or obsessive love, the kind we call 'out of control', which, in the words of Marlene Dietrich's song, makes us feel, 'I'm falling in love again, never wanted to, what am I to do, can't help it', has taken its place in the pantheon of romance as the crowning glory of love, as if the very fact that we think it to be 'out of control' defines it as 'true' love. Yet this kind of uncontrollable love is part and parcel of a general emotional process and open to the kind of manipulative techniques used in religion or in brainwashing.

Take one aspect of 'uncontrollable' love that we can all recognize, whether from our own experience or our observation of others. An individual 'falls in love' with someone who appears to all mutual friends either completely unsuitable or the absolute antithesis of the kind of person who would normally be thought lovable by that individual. One of the hallmarks of this particular kind of love is the lover's resistance to any outside appeals for common sense or thought, just as the experience of a mystical conversion is distinguished by its inaccessibility to rational argument.

Before Sargant, Freud described the same physical process, in *On the Theory of Hysterical Attacks*:

If an hysterical subject seeks intentionally to forget an experience or forcibly repudiates, inhibits and suppresses an intention or an idea, these psychical acts, as a consequence, enter the second state of consciousness; from there they produce their permanent effects and the memory of them returns as an hysterical attack.

He points out that it is the 'antithetic idea' that gains the upper hand as a result of general exhaustion, and comments:

It is owing to no chance coincidence that the hysterical deliria of nuns during the epidemics of the Middle Ages took the form of violent blasphemies and unbridled erotic language . . . it is the suppressed, the laboriously suppressed, groups of ideas that are brought into action in these cases by the operation of a sort of counter-will, when the subject has fallen a victim to hysterical exhaustion.

Clearly, because women far more than men are required by society to suppress a large proportion of their feelings, whether sexual, aggressive or simply strong, any prolonged excitation of the brain is likely to produce more 'ultra-paradoxical or antithetic' behaviour, simply because more is suppressed.

This is reflected in the fact that it is women, on the whole, who fall in love with 'unsuitable' men, whether because they are not from the proper social class or because the chosen men themselves treat the women badly in some way, and women who continue to defend their choices against all common sense, just as the religious will defend their faith.

So love itself is, at least in theory, something that could be consciously aroused in another by the careful manipulation of circumstances and of the person involved. The aim is to make the proposed lover over-excited, whether by extreme fright, grief, aggression or some other violent emotion, wait for the physical exhaustion and reap the harvest by being there and seeming powerful to the one who is now in a state of suggestibility. War itself creates these conditions and love affairs in wartime are notoriously both intense and ill-judged. And the very common day-dreams both men and women cherish about the moment their chosen one will actually choose them too – I rescue her from a burning house, I am wrecked with him upon a desert isle – combine proximity with hopes of gratitude and the element of drama that, unconsciously, they know could spark off the desired adoration.

Another method of creating what we might call, in schoolboy parlance, 'brain fag' is the one used in the puppy experiment to create dependence. Everyone who has observed anything about the workings of attraction has either deplored or exploited the fact that many people, particularly women, respond less fervently to a consistent and steady display of love than to the off-again, on-again, blow-hot, blow-cold treatment. Once more, the constant firing of the neutrons (to put it in bald physical terms) leads to a hiatus in which the conditions for a kind of new imprinting are present – it is, experts believe, similar to the state of brain activity in young children. All those who have either experienced or attempted to induce such sudden conversions or changes of mind, from the early mystics through to Wesley, Mesmer, William Sargant, Billy Graham or the Korean Mr Moon and his Moonies, have used one or more of the same techniques (furious excitation by music, drumming, hell-fire preaching, dancing or other strong emotional circumstances), induced the same reactions (exhaustion, fainting, trance, minor collapse) and achieved the same states of mind (an acceptance of hitherto alien beliefs that goes beyond rationality into unquestioning faith). Most significantly, there is a definite preponderance of women among those who are converted in this way. One of the Commissioners appointed by the French Royal Society of

Medicine in 1784 to investigate Mesmer's claims, remarked that the great majority of subjects who experienced the 'crisis' Mesmer aimed to bring about with his practice of 'animal magnetism' were women. The Commission later produced a private report for the King which pointed out the moral dangers of the 'magnetism' treatment for women, clearly hinting that such was the submissiveness and suggestibility of Mesmer's female patients that 'the crisis' also involved, at its last stage, 'the sweetest emotion', succeeded by 'languor, prostration and a sort of slumber of the senses'. Orgasm, we presume, had taken place, thus putting the females into dire peril of losing their cherished virginity and honour.

Of course, women are not alone in falling happy or unhappy victim to the brain excitation that can lead to love, though I would guess a higher proportion of women than men do so involuntarily and to their own injury. The poetry, songs and prose outpourings of men through the centuries tell us of their frequent enthralment by La Belle Dame sans Merci and I suspect that Richard Lovelace, in claiming that he had to go off and fight because 'I could not love thee, dear, so much, loved I not honour more', was unknowingly giving both himself and his 'dear' a boost of excited neutrons by putting some occasional distance between them.

Research work now being done hints at a similar state labelled 'non-specific arousal', which seems to accompany hormonal changes. Penelope Shuttle who wrote, with Peter Redgrove, *The Wise Wound,* a book on menstruation, mentions this experimental work and explains the state as one in which the mind is exquisitely receptive and can be changed into depression or creativity according to the surrounding circumstances. Mary Brown Parlee, in a recent article primarily concerned with menstruation, mentions the work of Schacter and Singer who found that when subjects were in a bodily state different from their normal one (produced in the experiment by an injection of epinephrine) they interpreted the way they felt by relying upon outside cues. Thus the state of non-specific arousal produced by the epinephrine was labelled 'happiness' when the subjects were in the presence of a cheerful companion who joked with them, but when the companion behaved in an angry and depressed fashion, subjects labelled the same non-specific state of arousal anger or depression. In other words, the availability of 'appropriate' labels – 'this is a depressing situation' – affected the way the subject labelled, and presumably the way he experienced, his altered bodily state.

This is not unlike the traditional preparation for taking hallucinogens. Any careful user of marijuana or LSD will lay great emphasis on his state of mind before using the drug, since the theory (and often the practice) is that if he is angry or depressed he will have a bad trip and if euphoric, a good one. So the hormonal changes that are present in altered bodily states link up with the more mechanical means used by mystics, witch doctors, hypnotists, preachers and psychologists in that the mechanics of everything from chanting to drugs produce the hormonal changes that increase suggestibility. It is not hard to guess that both the masked man and the young girl whom he seized from her car in February 1978 were in a state of intense emotional excitation and hormonal upheaval. Daniel Neito, kidnapper, and Giovanna Amati, kidnapped, fell in love; the fate, it seems, of an increasing number of female kidnappees. Perhaps the ancient Sicilian habit of abducting a recalcitrant bride was found to be as effective in arousing love as in putting paid to her virginity. Perhaps all the high love dramas of myths and sagas and literature, Romeo and Juliet, Dante and Beatrice, Tristan and Isolde, came about because the dramatic circumstances themselves imprinted the couples upon each other by actual cerebral changes so that, like conversion to a faith, nothing exterior and nothing rational could affect that love.

But, of course, this brain fever does not deserve the label love. The reasoning brain, the neo-cortex, is disbarred from this transaction, which takes place in the mammal brain. This brain may well be the source of some of the world's greatest works of art and music, probably by giving the creator access to the buried memories and hidden byways of the unconscious and possibly by heightening suggestibility in general. It cannot, however, give birth to a love based on the reality of another person. Once again, the word is lacking, once again 'love' represents a sort of trampoline, a launching pad into something else, usually as far away from the individual who appears to inspire it as it is possible to get. Konrad Lorenz's ducklings, we could say, 'loved' Lorenz because they followed him everywhere and showed every duckling sign of love; but we must then acknowledge that we are being anthropomorphic, attributing human feelings to ducklings. In fact, the word we should use, though humanity is not in the habit of allying itself so closely with the natural world, is animalomorphic, which in this case means attributing duckling feelings to humans – Koestler called it 'ratomorphic'. The ducklings have gone through the same process that Romeo went through with Juliet or Frau Stangl with her husband. The only difference is that ducklings haven't the additional nervous system that allows them to sing songs and poetry or to paint beautiful pictures of their loved one, Konrad Lorenz.

Art, in humans, is one of the very many side-effects of an imprinting process that sends some of the imprinted soaring to great heights, all in the name of 'love' or 'passion'. And very nice too, for the rest of us. But not always, one suspects, all that great for the loved one, the flesh and blood trampoline. Very many women have, of course, made their mark upon the world as living trampolines, 'inspirations' for great men, but there is an unreality in being an 'inspiration' that can leave the woman herself, the real person, lonely as a cloud. One thinks, at a less high-flown level, of such women as Marilyn Monroe, beloved of men in their millions because of the excitation and untouchability of her celluloid curves. What did all that hubbub have to do with her, the small sexless being inside those curves called Norma Jean?

The whole process of *falling* in love, as opposed to love, is to all intents and purposes a carbon copy, reproduced again and again until its writing almost fades into unreadability, of its original blueprint of behaviour between child and mother. To put the picture crudely, bodily needs in the infant set up a congestion of the nervous system which produces bodily communication – howls – and these are only relieved by the satisfaction of those bodily needs, when Mum arrives to feed. But the infant lives in a continual and fairly hellish world of the present; it has no idea, when it is wretched, that wretchedness will ever cease. Who is the arbiter of the end of wretchedness and the dawn of happiness? Mother. A great dim looming figure who is all-powerful, who is present during frantic states of excitation and who is, to the infant perception, totally unpredictable. The child cannot control her comings and her goings nor his own bliss or misery – it is all beyond him. Inside the brain little bursts of electricity are busy etching out a potentially lifelong pattern.

Although to fall in love may be an exhilarating experience that transforms every banality into something magical, or causes the most hideous anxieties and grief, it is, for all that, a relatively mundane process. If a man wished to make a particular woman fall in love with him (and it is easier that way round because women have less ego and a stronger preliminary conditioning) he would, in 1979, have no need of love potions or cabbalistic spells. His allies would be technology, neurology and brainwashing techniques and, given access to the appropriate surroundings and circumstances, his chances of success are pretty good.

What must he do? First, manage things so that he and the woman are thrown together more or less alone. It is important that the woman is cut off from friends, relatives and familiar surroundings and that the new surroundings are in some way threatening or strange. He should make her feel that only he is to be trusted, is not alien to her. He must then organize others to upset and humiliate her and arrange events to appear chaotic and without order, so that she becomes disorientated, unable to judge or discern what is actually happening. He himself must at times protect and comfort her and at other times ignore her or disappear from the scene for short periods. If he can also arrange for her to have to think herself physically unattractive, dirty, clumsy, so much the better, for then he can imply that she is all those things and only *he* does not mind, only *he* will take care of her despite her obvious drawbacks. A span of sleeplessness and a lot of continuous noise would help too. As she reacts to him with increasing dependency, he should reinforce that dependency with more tenderness. Occasionally, he must engineer a quarrel, show her brief violence and then beg for forgiveness. The climax must be an attempt to bring the woman to a state of extreme emotion, whether panic, fear, pain, exhaustion, awe, shock or great pleasure hardly matters. Upon her collapse she will, if he has performed correctly, be in love with him.

There is nothing new about this technique except its conscious application. All the classic settings for sudden passion incorporate something of it, from kidnappings and hijackings to holiday romance, from the dangers of the Capulet–Montague feud and the Tristan–Isolde elopement to the close confinement over a period of a shipboard idyll. Even those nationals who are famous for their attachment to their country – the Russians, the Irish – are conditioned into that attachment through the suffering those countries have inflicted upon them. One of the classic early brainwashings of woman by man is set out, step by step, in *The Taming of the Shrew* – denigration, abuse, disorientation, unfamiliarity, isolation from family, sleeplessness and, for eventual submission, rewards.

Whether or not a love thus engendered has any possibility of lasting is neither here nor there. This kind of love, like many other kinds, has no secure base in the reality of the beloved and is no more fit to last than a butterfly is fit to live after its purpose is finished.

SIX

The Purpose

'Love makes the world go round.'

Before we explore the future of love, before we can properly begin to imagine what it could become, we need to strip off all the veils of habit and usage, discard the frills of passion and romance and try to peer beyond at the bleak imperative that has always governed mankind's journey, an imperative shared with all other living things – survival. The question, in this case, is simple. In terms of the survival of our race, what is love for? A question that is, on the face of it, so vague and vast as to be bordering on idiocy. If there is one answer there are several hundred, but there is, at least, no harm in asking. Human beings have never been deterred from questioning by the possibility of getting no answers.

At any rate, if I condense the question to fit a biological framework, there may be some hope of an answer shimmering, however faintly, upon the horizon. The fact is that whatever we are, however we behave and every detail of the way we are shaped, all this personal luggage that we carry today is with us either because it has been tried, tested and found valuable for the better propagation of the species or, at the very least, nothing has proved it positively damaging as yet. Whether the particular behaviour, characteristics, physical traits or mental beliefs bring individuals happiness or unhappiness, whether they are deemed moral, immoral or amoral, is beside the point. The supreme test of evolution remains crystal clear through the ages. Whatever is alive has passed the test. Whatever is extinct has failed.

We, the human race, are very much alive and so, to date, we are a successful species. Nevertheless, we have very little reason to congratulate ourselves. Apart from anything else, as a species we are still so wet behind the ears, so recently emerged from the mists of time, that our viability has yet to be put to the test. Compare our few hours with the three whole days in which such a supposedly inferior form of life as the reptile, small, medium and quite shockingly large, dominated the earth and still survives, and it is immediately evident that we have no cause at all to rest on our laurels.

To rephrase the original question: what purpose does the emotion of love serve in keeping homo sapiens extant? Is it central or merely peripheral, just an accidental and unimportant icing on the essential cake? One fact suggests itself immediately. We all know, some of us to our bitter cost, that simply to reproduce ourselves requires nothing more than the uniting of the male and female genitals. If that is done, the fact that it is done with tenderness or the utmost violence is totally irrelevant for the purpose of survival of the species. And yet a form of love is in our repertoire of emotions and by its presence announces the possibility of some evolutionary purpose above or perhaps merely in combination with the older drive of sex. Why?

Practically speaking, the first essential requirement for love is the need, for reproductive purposes, of another member of the same species. This apparently obvious necessity was for countless eons deemed quite irrelevant by evolution. Life managed to produce more life in a way Narcissus might have envied – one living entity simply divided its nucleus and lo, there were two where one had been. A clean, efficient process that continues in simple forms to this day. An amoeba makes more amoebas by splitting interminably into carbon copies of itself and may, for all we know, continue this do-it-yourself cloning when the vast civilizations of homo sapiens are rubble and no naked ape is left to walk the earth.

Why then did this perfectly workable state of affairs ever change? Why was it necessary to introduce individual to individual in order to reproduce if the old way was perfectly satisfactory and gave evidence of its satisfactory nature by having survived at least one thousand million years? Heaven knows, life would have been a dullness that surpasses understanding but evolution, as far as we can ascertain, spares little thought for the quality of life and is chillingly uninterested in whether or not individual units find their allotted span entertaining or otherwise. Protozoa may not be fun things but they are with us still.

Luckily for us, natural selection operated upon some of our protozoan ancestors to force them out of one cosy niche into more foreign parts. It is as if Nature so deplored waste that, having managed to put together a whole planet complete with such desirable features as uplands and lowlands, deserts and jungles, hot climates and cold, and other mod. cons, she was damned if any part of it was going to remain empty for lack of pioneering flora and fauna. By producing carbon copies of organisms you ensure only that one particular ecological niche is ever more efficiently filled. To colonize a planet and make sure that a new environment does not wipe out life because that life is too meticulously fitted to the old habitat means that you must offer the possibility that life forms can adapt and that involves offering variety. Carbon-copy protozoa are fine in their place but if their place alters, if the temperature drops or rises a few degrees, if any one of a number of changes occurs in their habitat, the finely adapted protozoa turn out to be altogether too finely adapted and perish. Besides, the protozoan niche becomes overcrowded and, in the end, unsuitable for any life.

Reproduction with another member of the species, bringing together two lots of genes, ensures that the offspring are different, to however minute a degree, from the parents. Variety is literally the spice of life. Evolution, plus the environment, has the chance to pick and choose recruits for further colonization and better survival. The great Tyrannosaurus Rex ruled all about him for millions of years but his doom, paradoxically, was sealed in the very fact that he became too perfectly adapted to his surroundings. When the climate changed, he could not. There was no give in him. But as he lay dying in the festering Mesozoic swamps, his death throes were watched from high up in the trees, where tiny furry mammals were preparing themselves to descend, all danger past. They had left their options open, kept a low profile and they had fur that could cope with the changing temperatures. Life went on because, in the beginning, one organism got together with another to reproduce. Love had its primeval origins in the need to diversify in order to survive. Me Tarzan, you Jane, united we stand.

The next imperative, once the offspring appeared, properly sprinkled with a hodge-podge of genes, was that offspring's survival into adulthood so that it, too, could reproduce. In general, evolution seems to have picked two opposite extremes to accomplish this. One, species that produced so many offspring that some, at least – without any parental care – would slip through the myriad nets of danger and reach maturity. And, two, species that produced very few offspring and could therefore provide excellent parental care in their defence and nourishment. Both methods have worked well. Indeed, for the purposes of long-term survival it may turn out that the quantity method is the more successful but, since love as an evolutionary tool is the subject, we must leave the quantity method here. Sticklebacks, herring and frogs cannot be said, by even the most anthropomorphic amongst us, to display anything remotely resembling love for their clouds of eggs. Easy come, easy go. What little they do for their offspring's defence and growth is programmed from birth.

Things are necessarily more emotional for the more adaptable species. The trick of adaptation is to have less programming in your genes for ritualistic or instinctual behaviour and more inherent possibilities for learning behaviour. And if the infant has to learn rather than merely act out of instinct, then it follows that the learning is going to take some time and require experienced adults of some goodwill to teach. The mother of the infant is nearest to hand and the rest of the tribe are necessary for the infant's socialization and defence. A sort of affection, a kind of patience, once shown, is selected by evolution as useful for survival and therefore those species that exhibit it will flourish. The infant has its own armoury of traits, selected because they arouse protectiveness in adults (see Chapter 5) and it is obvious that one of the most important reasons for the evolutionary development of a kind of loving had to do with the fact that infants who needed a prolonged learning period were forced to rely on a certain amount of altruism from otherwise aggressive and competitive adults if the species were to survive.

But the growth of even this love seems to have been dependent, for many millennia, on its Janus face – hate. Or rather, to be a little more dispassionate about it, to know your friends is easier when you have enemies, if only in the most basic sense that friends don't eat you and enemies do. Everyone has some memory of childish 'secret societies', those warm enclaves in sheds and tree houses where the main purpose of gathering together three or more was to draw up elaborate rules for keeping other children out. If enemies do not exist, then in the cause of creating solidarity they must be invented and, once invented, they will be feared. It is possible that even the ability to distinguish your friends is dependent on the negative talent for distinguishing your enemies. Not-friend came before friend. Your not-not-friend was, by definition, your friend.

In the animal world, this tendency can be seen in full force. Gibbons live in family groups and reinforce those ties by setting up, every dawn, an incredible racket, howling and shrieking across the trees to make sure every other gibbon family for miles around knows of their existence and, approximately, their habitat and numbers. Then they spend a full hour in a myriad phoney wars, rushing about after each other, taunting and testing and generally making hullabaloo, all in the interests of heightening tension towards the outside world and creating intimacy on the domestic front. Herring gulls court by conjuring up imaginary enemies, carrying out the full ritual of aggression towards a mirage and then, well set up by adrenalin and self-satisfaction after this pantomime, go off and mate. The whole territorial mechanism, once believed to be solely in aid of retaining enough land to provide food for a tribe or a couple, may well boil down to this same creation of enemies. We have colonized this area, you are stepping over the borders, therefore we can battle with you, therefore those who battle with us against you are our friends. There remain, in the languages of some primitive tribes of homo sapiens today, traces of words that show us the same inherent tendency, tribes who employ their word for 'human being' or 'man' only to describe themselves – every other human being is, to them, non-human, not even the same species as themselves.

All this is obvious enough if you think about it. Merely to imagine yourself, stripped of all money and possessions and deposited in the middle of an African veldt where the night ululates with strange sounds and every snapping twig signals danger is to grasp something of the priorities of all animals and earliest men – fear is the paramount emotion, survival the overriding drive and your only hope is to team up with your own species who are not likely actually to kill you. Ability to get along with them would become a prime necessity and, once learned, a valuable heritage to pass to offspring. For many eons, people who needed people were not just the luckiest people in the world, they were the only people in the world. Alone, you were a dead duck.

Getting along with, fitting in with others, offering small services in return for small services, picking fleas out of another's hair so that they would do the same for you was quite literally life itself, as we can see if we watch two apes grooming each other, buffaloes forming their formidable circle of defence or two cats cleaning each other's ears. Love it was not, as we guess at love, but an ancestor of that emotion it was and a vital one at that, bred from primeval terror and the constant threat of violent death.

So absolute is this ruling fear that it is now thought to hold first place in the newborn, overriding that more obvious need for food. In one famous experiment, baby macaque monkeys were separated from their mothers at birth and given a choice of dummy mummies, one made of wire with a built-in milk supply and the other a nice, soft, comforting shape without any milk. The infants immediately chose the soft dummy and spent their time clinging to it, leaving only to drink from the wire dummy. What's more, it became clear that the infants regarded the soft dummy not only as comforting but as a shelter in trouble. When frightened, they leapt for the soft dummy and clung there, appearing to derive confidence from its warmth and softness, even though the dummy itself did nothing for their protection, was completely unresponsive to them and gave no signals to prompt their behaviour. The experiments seem to prove that the desire to cling to something warm is paramount and lies in the infant's genetic code at birth, taking precedence over hunger and triggered by fear. Love is something soft and warm in time of trouble.

All kinds of human experience testify to the close link between love and fear. The games mothers play with their children, the peek-a-boos, the tickling, the throwing in the air, the hide-and-seeks are all unconsciously designed to strengthen ties by inducing fear, even when both emotions are aroused by the same person. Look, I will frighten you but look, I shall comfort you, too. One of the most poignant sights of childhood is the toddler howling wretchedly at something its mother has done while clinging grimly to the hand of its tormentor. Nor is the technique, if one can call anything so instinctive a technique, abandoned once childhood has passed. Many adults may glimpse the same mechanism at work in their own behaviour to lovers. Blowing hot and cold is one name for the process and an old racial and familial memory is stirred in us at such behaviour, strengthening our love, for good or evil. As we have seen, the brain itself works on much the same premise, at a physical level. Like everything else, this strong survival instinct can be mightily abused, reducing the lover to near-childish dependence which, in itself, because the tension has been so reduced, militates against the future relationship. Even such extremes as sadism and masochism are presumably grown from the same roots.

Nevertheless, there is no reason to think that an early kind of bonding among primates and the great apes was suddenly transformed into a higher emotion the moment the first hominid emerged on two legs. It seems clear that any form of romantic, individualized love between men and women is an extremely late arrival on the human scene. Preceding it by thousands of years is the bond between mother and child, created out of fear and strengthened through nourishment and endless little services. Even when homo sapiens appeared upon the earth nothing much in the way of a deeper sexually linked emotion took place for many centuries, unless we imagine that our earliest ancestors were somehow in advance of their descendants in recorded history. The male's role was probably a simple matter of impregnation, the soothing, if you like, of a mutual itch that had, in the minds of those who itched, nothing at all to do with the later appearance of an infant. So separate, in fact, was the initial deed from the eventual outcome that some primitive tribes today are only hazily aware of a connection and, in that, are not so different from many gents in grey flannel suits who walk the streets of, say, New York. These urban species know how babies are made but in their actions reveal the ancient human difficulty of connection, often showing every sign of primeval shock when it is revealed to them by a woman with whom they have 'mated' that she is pregnant. The whole history of abortion testifies to the fact that even women, the bearers of the infants, have certain problems in realizing intellectually that intercourse today may mean a baby in nine months' time.

Which brings us to a question that concerns us more closely even than the love between mother and child. What purpose does love serve between men and women? Since the sexual drive alone is quite sufficient to propagate the race and has served even the 'highest' animals efficiently to this day, why should love ever have evolved as an evolutionary tool? Is it, perhaps, a mere overspill from essential infant bonds or an evolutionary dead end, a side-effect of the new brain of homo sapiens that may, in the course of time, turn out to be actually destructive? Certainly, the growth of love – as opposed to a reasonable dose of nurture and social behaviour – seems in an odd way not only unnecessary but, at times, positively dangerous. Why should a species evolve an emotion that today actually *excludes* all other male and female members of the species on peril, at times, of their lives? If we, as a species, survive by being gregarious, why introduce an element that could so thoroughly divide one human being from another? Surely a sort of generalized affection, the kind of 'fitting in' managed by a primate, given a boost by the sex act, would not only have been sufficient but a more effective way to maintain low-key bonds without the superfluous threat of jealousy and a potentially destructive passion. All is fair in love and war is just a way of saying all is *unfair* in love and war, and those are certainly the two activities that most distinguish us from our nearest animal relatives. Animals discover no evolutionary imperative in fighting to the death or loving to the death, though both are human proclivities: are they merely evolutionary cul-de-sacs? Have we survived – and survived in plenty – because they are an essential part of our equipment or because we have managed in spite of them?

Here, the plot thickens almost to impenetrability. There is, to begin with, the theory of the eternal pregnancy of the human female, which rendered her vulnerable and in need of male protection, since she was unable either to protect herself or get food for her offspring. Therefore any bond that could keep one male interested in her individual fate and therefore the fate of her progeny would have had evolutionary backing. According to those, including Dr Desmond Morris, who hold this theory, the female had to alter the whole of her body in order to ensure this – the first of the sexual tricks designed to 'hold your man'. Face-to-face intercourse became essential to strengthen the bond over and above the ordinary promiscuous sexual drive because only by looking into the face while fucking could you mimic and capitalize on the mother/child bond and begin to know the individual from, as it were, the faceless bottom of old-style mounting. To achieve this, Dr Morris claims that the female shifted her erogenous zones from the back to the front so that the important sexual signals were on the same side as the eyes and the face instead of behind. So two rounded buttocks were copied by two rounded breasts (instead of the flat nipples of simian equipment), the lips became marked out and pink to fool the unwary male into thinking this was the reddened oestrus area and lo, the missionary position became *de rigueur*, with all its concomitant bonding by eyeball to eyeball contact in the sexual act, rather like an adult form of imprinting or the opposite of aversion therapy – boy, this is good and it's you I'm staring at while I'm feeling good. Only by doing this, goes the theory, can the male be seduced into rushing off and bringing back the bacon for the pregnant female and her brood.

An extraordinary theory in many ways, not least in its assumption that the female had, over the generations, to alter her whole body in order to buy her meal ticket with her new breasts, rather than developing her skills at foraging for her own food. Added to this, Morris theorizes that the female also had to discard her on-again-off-again monthly cycle inherited from the apes and become constantly receptive to the male so that the couple could fuck at any time and strengthen the individual bond between them. She was, he says, rewarded with the orgasm for this feat and both had their sex drive amplified above all other animals for the purpose of keeping them together throughout the infancy of their offspring.

There are so many doubtful and unbelievable aspects to this theory that it is hard to know where to begin. For a start, it is difficult to imagine that the female body would alter so radically in response to male sexual needs when the overriding concern of the female – and indeed the race – was for the infants. Elaine Morgan in *The Descent of Woman* explains the human female's rounded breasts, as well as other features such as the relative hairlessness of the body and the continuation of hair on the head, as results of the needs of infants rather than of adult males. Though holes can be picked in the minutiae of her theories, the basic assumption makes far more sense in terms of animals and evolution generally. Reproduction is the essential; female appearance and behaviour moulded itself to this fact and males followed behind.

Ah, but what of the female's vulnerability during pregnancy and her need for food for herself and her infants? Even the female cheetah – who mates and discards the male – slows down on the hunt as she gets heavier in pregnancy and often spends the last weeks hungry, besides losing at least one of her three or so offspring to predators while she is absent foraging for them after they are born. Apart from the fact that, in spite of the apparent difficulties, the tribe of cheetahs is still upon this earth, there are other theories that undermine the widely accepted idea that the male hunted for the female and had to ensure her 'faithfulness' while he was away by an individual bond.

Why would he require this monogamy before he understood paternity and long before the concept of property had entered his head, to make him want to be sure of his own descendants?

It seems at least as reasonable to assume that, like her female primate cousins, early woman was not the helpless victim of biological destiny that she was to become under the patriarchal system. She could have remained largely vegetarian and foraged for roots and berries for herself, as women in primitive tribes still do today, perhaps discovering fire as she went, to keep dangerous animals at bay, and raising the first crops from the seeds she scattered. Many female animals, including all herbivores and some carnivores like the lioness and the cheetah, manage to feed themselves throughout pregnancy and provide food for their young.

So the idea of an individualized love bond between man and woman having its source in the woman's need for sustenance and protection during pregnancy seems doubtful. Indeed, you could say that monogamy itself – considered so peculiarly and blessedly human by such institutions as the Church and capitalism in general – is actually a lower form of social development, since most of the more complex and intelligent mammals have rejected it in favour of looser tribal arrangements.

As for the human female exchanging the periodic oestrus for constant availability as a device to strengthen bonds between couples, there seems to be only the most tenuous evidence for it. Hard to believe that early woman had her reward in orgasm when, some thousands of years later, her descendants are still having trouble 'achieving' the Big O in spite of liberated men's best efforts. Nor does it seem sensible to interpret the heightened male sex drive in terms of some sort of hopeful monogamy. A whole spectrum of animal life, from the greylag goose to the gibbon, takes lifetime partners without any such sexual bonus and it can as well be argued that man's increased sexuality militated *against* monogamy rather than for it, since we know perfectly well that human nature today is not outstanding for its fidelity to one sexual object. Throughout 'civilized' history it has taken all the power, threats and punishments of governments and Church to keep man sexually faithful or even *with* his mate for any length of time. When you have to be threatened with horrors in this world and the next for the crime of adultery, can you assume that mankind's round-the-clock sexuality evolved solely in order to establish individual and lifelong bonds?

In my reading I have come across no studies of the possible psychological make-up of primitive man. Leakey's discovery of the skull of a little lady who lived a million years ago in the Transvaal gorge tells us nothing of what went on within that skull. In his novel *The Inheritors*, about a tribe of Neanderthalers, William Golding probably makes as good a guess as any anthropologist at the cloudy emotions and first faint tendrils of thought and memory. But the records we have of travellers, missionaries and anthropologists who have lived with and studied primitive tribes, some of whom exist today in much the same way as Leakey's lady, give us clues. Though there is an infinite variety of ritual and gods, of taboos and temperament and culture, there are some underlying similarities common to all that link 'modern' primitives with our earliest forefathers.

Anthropologists report that primitive man today often has no word in the language for 'I', only phrases meaning 'my people' that include himself. One writer tells of a missionary who commented on the sins of the people with whom he was interfering at the time. They are liars, he said. He had asked one noble savage who owned a certain house and piece of land and the man had responded with a sweeping gesture, saying that it belonged to him. The wretched missionary, imbued with individualism and ideas of private property, chastized the liar because he was unable to comprehend the true meaning. The house and land belonged to the tribe and the tribe was the man.

Love as we know it, the individualized emotional tie

between one human being and another and particularly between one woman and one man, had no relevance and therefore no place in the sparse equipment of primitive life. Again and again, anthropologists report the astonishment shown by tribal people at our assumption that a particular man or woman, husband or wife, is irreplaceable, unique or to be loved above others. If one member of a tribe does not see himself as unique, how shall he see another member as such? If 'I' means 'all of us', how can 'you' mean more? One man, noticing the distress of a white friend, asked the cause and was told he had just lost his wife. He showed much surprise at this over-reaction, saying, 'Well then, you must get another wife.'

Least of all is the practice of monogamy any evidence of the birth of love. Monogamy had to do with the male discovery of his part in creating the child, his ensuing desire to make sure of paternity by enforcing monogamy upon the woman with rites and sacraments. And the purpose of all this? The idea of property had entered his mind, the idea of dynasty and increasing wealth, an aim only to be achieved by 'owning' a woman's body, to the exclusion of every other male. That 'love' had anything to do with this male possession of female property would have seemed absurd to both parties and continues to seem so right up to our own times in many parts of the world. That the practice of monogamy – marriage – was not based on love does not preclude it but is in no way essentially connected to it. You do not put two prisoners in a cell in the hope that they will grow to like each other, though they may, more in spite of their mutual incarceration than because of it.

Nevertheless, a sort of love did come into being, for good or for evil. Its first tentative growth was fertilized by the wealth and leisure of a burgeoning aristocracy in the first city-states of Mesopotamia, Sumer, Egypt and, later, Greece. Then, it was essentially an anarchic and elitist emotion, making no obvious contributions to either State or family and at times even contrary to the best interests of both. Peasants had no time to spare for such frivolity.

The Greek of the fifth century BC did not direct his love at his wife, who was there only to run his household, bear his children and assure his immortality, by God and Mammon. With time on his hands and temporal power to give him a new and pleasurable sensation of his own uniqueness, he turned with a fine contempt for his own carefully erected institutions to falling in love with pretty boys and those women who had something rather more immediate to offer than heirs. At last man – if not woman – had time and money to play and love was as good a game as any. And, oddly, love was born out of that first consciousness of self, of individual autonomy. What a paradox. Before the mind of man had grasped his separateness from all other men, he was not separate. He did not need to be reminded that the bell tolled for him any more than we would need to have it pointed out to us that a wound to a finger is a wound to the body. Individual love was irrelevant, just as it is irrelevant to an infant who has no choice but to be a part of its mother. Deeper than any conscious wish to love her, the child *is* her because every instinct tells it the impossibility of survival without her.

But as man began to gather together in increasing numbers, in city-states, as he began to divide from his fellows and pigeon-hole himself – the one into a different class, the other into a different job – as it became impossible to know each person in the crowds upon the streets, human beings were slowly forced to learn the beginnings of sep-arateness. A man could die in the city and you would not know it. A child could be born and the news would only reach a few. Strange faces were everywhere. For the first time, human beings experienced loneliness, the loneliness of the crowd. No place in that larger society was your place from birth, destined for you as a vital limb of the group. You had, in a way never contemplated before, to make your place and that involved realizing separateness, individuality.

Isolation terrified. Now a human being was confined within the perimeter of his own body, defined by that out-line, cut off from the myriad limbs and heads that once were his own. In a small group, men lived like ants, the image – curiously – so often and so inaccurately used of men in modern metropolises. To comprehend the behaviour of individual ants within an anthill or, for that matter, bees within a beehive, they must be thought of as a single organism, linked by a million nerve-endings and endocrinal messages, that happens to have each segment very slightly separated, like an eel that is suddenly chopped into pieces and yet continues to wriggle on the fishmonger's slab as if it were whole. In vast modern cities humans have nothing of the closeness of ants, no messages unite them, no nerves bridge the gap between one entity and another. Each goes his own way, without any innate knowledge of the anthill's needs, without a single unifying aim.

Engulfed by the weight of himself, the burden of individuality that had shifted to his shoulders, he began to make desperate efforts to join himself again, at least to one other human being. The whole refrain of love has this chorus. To be one flesh. To be part of another. To have two hearts beat as one. You are me, I am you, I am yours, you are mine. Religions were invented with one basic motive – whether Moslem, Hindu, Buddhist or Christian – to be 'at one' with God, to have God take us, to be united with Him, to give ourselves to God. The lost garden of Eden, the ancient dreams of Paradise are the memories of unity before the casting out, before the knowledge of our separate nakedness. Before the apple, Eve was Adam and Adam Eve. Protestations of love were irrelevant, you may love yourself but you do not tell yourself so. After the apple of knowledge, you look from within your own skull at others, cut off from you, and you observe that they are different, alien. From then on, you must strive to find a bridge that will give you, once again, access to the old Utopia of belonging without thought, and love is the bridge, sex the scaffolding of that bridge. Between the bridge, the penis, and the arched supports, the vagina, the cut-off self attempts to join the other.

The story of birth and growth, each time it occurs, is another microcosmic re-enactment of unity and later separation. Mother and foetus are one flesh, intricately meshed in skin and bone and blood. Expulsion from the womb is the first separation, the slow learning process of each infant the second. From utter dependence the child learns and each lesson is his alone, not to be duplicated by any other infant anywhere else in the world. In the end, he is what he has learned and therefore is separate from his mother and, in today's society, from all other human beings. He regards the world and others in it out of a matrix that is uniquely his and yet he yearns to be the same, to engulf another human being's experience as a cannibal ate human flesh in the belief that only thus would he acquire that flesh-experience and skill. I could eat you, says the lover.

Pretty imagery? Metaphysical fantasy? Yes, all of that and all of it an attempt by the new brain of humanity to encompass the burden of consciousness that can, if it has the courage, grasp the evolutionary reasons for what the brain tucked underneath the neo-cortex feels, that old mammal brain of clouded unsorted emotions. From the moment evolution decided that carbon copies gave it no choice and made the first offspring from two separate cells the aim has been the same. More diversity. More and more and more. The ever-increasing complexity of human societies, the vast discoveries, even those discoveries that seem the most to threaten our very existence, make diversity ever more essential if we are to survive. Strangely, the evolving morality of man that is so often cited by reactionaries as contrary to Nature – the maturing tendency, for instance, to care for the weak who would otherwise fall by the wayside or to tolerate the extremes of human behaviour, the freaks, the non-conformists, the extremists – has its basis in this necessity for diversity. Pacifists provide a possibility of natural selection against the aggressive (they are, after all, alive at the end of wars to breed). The promiscuous offer up their genes to balance the monogamists. The ambitious are counteracted by the non-competitive. The more society imposes conformity upon its members, the more the fringe people, the misfits, are important. They offer a way out for evolution if things go wrong. They are a bolt-hole, an emergency door, an escape hatch from the sudden downward spiral to doom. In all human societies, however small, there have always been misfits. In the aggressive society of the Doby Islanders, a timid man is diversity. In the mild communes of Samoa, aggression is rare but valuable. There are many ways of living for human beings and that species to which we belong has raised diversity to greater heights than any other.

The price is high, survival is the aim and love, an overflow from parental drives, the consolation. Because surely one of the uses for love between adults is as a soothing balm to the troubled neo-cortex, that lonely consciousness that mourns its isolation, fears its own death and is not yet equipped to see what purpose, if any, such self-awareness serves. We alone of all the species on earth know that there is tomorrow and tomorrow and tomorrow and that knowledge, which is in many ways our blessing, is also our curse. We ask ourselves why we are here and there is no answer, but love softens those bruising edges. Love seems to give us a reason for living and any emotion that succeeds in doing this is a natural for selection.

Out of aboriginal darkness came co-operation, reciprocity; out of the infant's helplessness and fear came affection and protection and so humanity began the long journey that may end in true adult love. In our own time, love is only half-evolved, it fulfils most of our ancient needs but has not yet grown to encompass what we most badly need to face the future. Another kind of love is slowly becoming an evolutionary necessity if we are to mature upon our old home planet and that puts love, for the first time, squarely at the heart of the survival stakes, no longer the icing on the cake but the cake itself. And that, I think, is where women come on to centre stage.

SEVEN

The Psyche

'There'll be some changes made . . .'

Every female child born on this earth within recorded history has had to absorb one fact. She is a member of that half of the human race considered inferior to the other half. The small cleft that marks her off from her brother is not merely a difference, it is the stamp of the sub-standard. Whatever the circumstances of her birth, whatever genetic endowment she inherits, whether she is born heiress to a fortune in money, talent or physical beauty, even heiress to a throne, a long shadow falls across her, the shadow of the second sex. However much she struggles, however she succeeds, that shadow must touch some part of her and deform.

Of course, all human beings are misshapen in some way: the newborn infant has to take its chances in the society of its birth and every influence that comes to bear upon it, whether personal, social, economic, religious, whether happy or calamitous, will suppress some tendencies and heighten others. That is an intrinsic part of being alive. But I think it fair enough to say that the female child suffers a more rigid shaping, one that forces her to conform more closely to a stereotype. Men are distorted by virtue of the role set for their sex but because they belong to the dominant sex they have more room for manoeuvre, more ways in which to push their own individuality through the restrictions of that role, more space to breathe more deeply. Whatever their handicaps, efforts to break out of the mould are considered at least respectable, if not necessarily rewarded. Women, on the other hand, are historically penalized for the same efforts and their rewards come only from remaining (and even looking) as much like the stereotype as possible. In a very general way, then, the female sex has been forced away from the main pull of evolution – diversity – and pushed into conformity.

The loss, so far, to the race as a whole is incalculable.

But now, at last, there are signs of change. Women are gaining control over the reproductive processes that were always a major restriction upon their lives. The control is by no means complete and often bitterly opposed but victory, I hope, is inevitable, however artificially postponed. And as a result, we are increasingly able to be financially independent, an ability as necessary in a socialist as in a capitalist society because whether work is rewarded in coin or according to need, we can become self-sufficient. No longer will we need a member of the opposite sex to get a roof over our heads, food in our bellies or status in our world and from such external factors, combined with all that we have learnt as dependents, will come the vital internal changes in the very structure of our souls, our egos, ourselves. And once women have changed, can men be far behind?

It is often taken for granted that the inner springs of human motivation and behaviour cannot change, have been essentially the same since Ramopithecus swung down from the trees and reared up on his back legs. 'That's human nature for you,' they say. 'You can't change human nature.' What they really mean, I imagine, is that you can't change animal nature and anyone who has watched a dog carefully circle round and round upon his plump terylene-filled plastic-covered cushion to press down some ancient memory of primeval grass will sympathize, even though the dog itself has a muzzle so blunted by men's manipulations that it can hardly breathe and would last not a second in a chase across that primeval grass. Remnants of animal behaviour keep mankind in his proper place to this day or, more sadly, push him into an improper place as a destructive Lord of Creation, but the fact remains that we regard ourselves, since Freud's great minings, as having a unique inner structure, composed vaguely of unconscious desires, conscious prohibitions upon those desires and a rag-bag of other layers, from childhood repressions to some sort of 'spirit' or 'soul', all of which we deem to have been eternally human. Perhaps this belief gives us a sense of continuity, perhaps our species has been so short a time upon earth that we are unable to imagine that something so profound as our inner motivations could have changed during that mere blink of an eyelid.

But all the evidence is otherwise, in spite of many psychiatrists' continuing insistence on considering the individual as if he came from no particular society, no unique personal background, no special time slot, had gathered no moss from social pressures or mores and therefore explaining all neuroses, aberrations, anxieties and twitches in exactly the same way, whether the 'patient' under study is a Pakistani woman from a rural village or an old Etonian.

Men of other disciplines have been more perceptive. Anthropologists agree on the tribal psyche of primitive man (Chapter 6). Oswald Spengler, in *The Decline of the West,* posited two types of masculine psyche: the Apollonian man of the classical world and Faustian man of the modern world. To the Apollonian, the idea of an inward development of personality was alien. He saw life as a pleasant landscape which was threatened only from the outside by random and brutal events causing havoc to the unlucky. Faustian man, on the other hand, sees the same catastrophes as inevitable culminations of past choices and experiences arising from the inner life.

Nietzsche divided men into the Dionysian, who finds the value of life through escaping from the boundaries of his five senses, and the Apollonian middle-of-the-roader, who operates within known boundaries and refuses to meddle with anything that might rock the inner boat. Spengler and Nietzsche are among many who recognize not only that there are different psychological types but that these differences are, to a very great extent, formed by the necessities and limitations of history and economic development. Fred Weinstein and Gerald Platt argue in their recent book *The Wish to be Free* that before the industrial revolution child-rearing was a family project, unrelated to specific sexually differentiated roles, so the child internalized his parents as a 'collective unit' and developed 'a less complex and less differentiated superego structure' than his modern counterpart. Without a father who provided some model of abstract authority, the child could not, they say, have developed the abstract quality that allows for the implementation of personal morality and the relaxation of external controls.

In other words, before the industrial revolution, there was no Oedipus complex. When that revolution came, iron entered life and the soul. Division of labour became a norm – where once a man had started, overseen and finished a job, now he more profitably performed one task on a conveyor belt, a cog in a larger machine. Extended families broke up in the move from country to town and each worker was defined by his wages. The family dwindled from a large amorphous crowd of parents, grandparents, aunts, uncles and children to one man, one woman and their offspring. Links with the outside community withered, the old country festivals and the mutual dependencies of the village were left behind. Working life now was a hard, uncreative and separate thing, a slog with only one satisfaction – the money at the end of the day – and the family, wife and children, came to be seen as the only refuge from the cold, uncaring world outside. In time, with increasing isolation and prosperity, another and final division of labour took place. The woman stayed alone at home as a full-time unpaid mother, the man went out alone and earned the bread.

Shut into a family that contained only an authoritative and usually absent father, an ever-present but non-authoritative mother and some brothers and sisters, surrounded by a world that rewarded few virtues but monetary success, each son could only identify with the father, since there were no other models, but in doing so the struggle for his own identity – essential for the market-place – became fiercer. Thus, in the Oedipal struggle, the mould of modern man's inner structure was laid down. Men discovered the inner life and abandoned the old pleasure–pain behaviourism for the dynamics of internalized obedience, the father's outer voice that became the inner conscience. And when Freud revealed the demands of the individual for autonomy on a personal and familial level and 'the rights of the ego within the individual', these demands reflected the current struggle for equal political rights and unfettered competition in the economic arena, just as all other inner changes had either preceded or reflected outer political and economic change.

The price for this inner journey was high, its greatest cost a pervading loneliness and alienation; the beginnings of that twentieth-century dis-ease, stress; an increasing competitiveness and materialism to fill an inner vacuum and the pitting of individual success against the general good. Set against that came the realization that hierarchy could be rejected for democracy and dependency for individual autonomy. It is a journey now accepted and undertaken by men everywhere who are well-fed enough to be able to bother with inner journeys at all.

Woman, however, has been forced to take a different path. Her role has remained static and constant throughout the ages – wifehood, the servicing of men, and motherhood, the servicing of children. In our time, the image of motherhood given by Christianity is selfless, sacrificial and that sacrifice is for men. A mother is not just a female of the species who has performed a natural function, one among others, and given birth. No. Her mother-role is made larger than life, mythic, tinged with melancholy and a kind of apprehension. The more religious the work of art, the sculpture or the painting, the more luminously glum the madonna looks, a type of upper servant who has been entrusted, rather against men's judgment, with the transient care of a precious object belonging to others more important than herself. Worse, she appears to suspect that her charge will one day be the death of her, will ask, 'Woman, who art thou to me?' Mary, virgin selected by a VIP to be the vessel by which another VIP is born. And what are we doing down on our knees in front of this emblem of our culture? We are worshipping the birth of a man-child. Recently, we have shown a little audacity. We have drawn cartoons of a man running out of a stable and shouting, 'It's a girl.' Worth a giggle but the laughter springs from the nervousness of blasphemy against God and against Nature. The natural object for gentle, warm, protective and proud motherhood is a son.

So a young girl, looking at these images, feeling their power, knows herself to be the outsider. She is not a part of that cosy holy circle, father, mother, son. There they are, figures in a Christmas crèche, Joseph standing protectively over the woman who bows protectively over a boy. Mary is merely the token woman in the real Trinity – Father, Son and Holy Ghost. The girl, pressing her nose against the window, has no part in this except, herself, to become a son's mother – preferably as virginally as possible. And yet, being a mere female, she is an imperfect vessel and may one day produce – out of a sort of deformation of her reproductive mechanism – a daughter instead.

I have a vision of labouring women, bodies on a rack, sweat pouring, knuckles white, surrounded by whispering women, the men outside. And then, joy, the first tiny cry. Smiles spread across every face and if the midwife then announces, face glowing, 'It's a boy!' the smiles broaden, laughter breaks out, the men come in and clap the father on the back, he radiates pride, everyone radiates pride. But if the midwife must say the baby is a girl even the fondest husband, even today, hesitates a fraction of a second before he rallies, everyone hesitates. Then the claps on the back, the smiles are heartier than before, to cover that tiny moment when they all, even the mother, felt let down. She cradles the girl baby tenderly, protectively. It is more flesh of her flesh than a boy would be but since she knows her flesh is inferior, she is not proud. This baby is not the world's baby, only hers.

Through a large part of history, the birth of a girl was something approaching catastrophe for the mother. Her husband's virility was at stake. The old Jewish proverb runs 'a man is not a man until he has a son', a son who can fulfil his hope of handing down his name, keeping his property flourishing, his lands husbanded. In many societies a man was – and still is – allowed to repudiate a wife who was either barren or produced only daughters. The two are considered much alike. Girls historically required dowries to shift them from their fathers' hands and even today remnants of that dowry practice remain. The fathers of many daughters groan under the weight of paying large sums for marriage ceremonies. In Roman times, girl babies were often exposed, left on bare mountainsides to die of hunger or vultures' attacks. Sometimes the mother was expected to anoint her nipples with poison, draw the baby girl to suck and watch the poison work. These customs, arising as they did out of the low value of women in society, have left their mark.

The classic Freudian view of a little girl's voyage to self-realization is one fraught with dangers which, often, she only partly manages to circumnavigate and thus only partly matures, as compared with her brother. The voyage is well-mapped. First horror – she discovers she has no penis, that she *is* castrated, whereas the boy merely fears castration. Next, she has to give up the hope of 'having' or impregnating her mother and, imagining that this is her mother's fault for refusing to supply her with a penis, transfers her affections to her father, converts the wish for a penis into the wish for a child and becomes passive, sexually, where once she was active. The rest of her life is spent compensating for the lack of a penis, an oddly frustrated, unsatisfied creature of whom Freud asked, 'What do women want?' Her brother, on the other hand, wanting to possess his mother and afraid that his father will castrate him for that desire, ruthlessly suppresses it, accepts his father's authority and, with it, the authority and mores of his society. He builds a strong super-ego, authority's internal voice called conscience, thus fitting himself snugly into the community. His sister, who has no such pressure on her to repress her father-fixation but only to shift it, at the appropriate time, slightly sideways on to a husband, cannot do such a good job on her super-ego, so that it is, in Freud's own words, 'never so inexorable, so impersonal, so independent of its emotional origins as we require it to be in men'. To put it in more general terms: man is moral, woman amoral, man an insider, woman an outsider, man the ruler, woman his subject. And the results are what we know as 'feminine' characteristics – a woman is less competitive, more dependent on the approval of others, less strongly influenced by abstract codes of behaviour, more emotional, more loving and more maternal.

And very nice too. But before we go on to wonder whether a super-ego is worth having, it might be as well to look at some of the theories that attack Freud's view at the roots.

Feminists, lay and academic, have spent much of their time over the past decade pointing out that Freud's central issue in the formation of women's psyches – penis envy – was not a symbolic but a downright practical envy, rooted in fact. If a boy is only perceived by his sister as different from her by his possession of a penis and yet is clearly treated as a more important being than herself, a fact reflected in the adult world as well, then it is hardly surprising that she comes to the conclusion that a penis is what entitles you to this preferential treatment and envies it. So equal out the positions of the sexes and you will have ended her envy and set her on the path to a liberated adulthood. And anyway, who was to say that boys did not suffer from 'womb envy' and spend the rest of their psychic lives trying to compensate for their inability to have children?

Meanwhile other theories have entered the field of battle, more recent than the spate of argument that followed in Freud's wake, from Melanie Klein's account of a distinct, separate and vaginally centred feminine experience to Karen Horney's belief that the shift away from the girl's initial attachment to her mother and its replacement with her father was only a natural principle founded upon the attraction between the sexes. The French analyst, Jacques Lacan, himself a Freudian, proffers the view – based on new ideas of language formation – that since the newborn infant perceives itself as at one with the universe it can only become a communicating and sexed individual as it discovers 'difference'. First, it must split off from its mother and form an image of itself so that language becomes necessary to make demands and then, on seeing a penis, both sexes take the next step into a gender identity. His theory, because it emphasizes the penis only as a symbol of difference and not of an inherent superiority (society alone invests 'difference' with values), is distinctly more encouraging for women, though what happens to girl infants who never glimpse a penis is not explained by any psychologist.

In *The Rocking of the Cradle and the Ruling of the World* Dorothy Dinnerstein suggests that if men and women were held equally responsible for the earliest care of the infant, not in the patchy experimental way now happening here and there in the West, but on a vast scale as the accepted mode of child-rearing, then the whole inner structure of human beings would be radically altered, with far-reaching implications for everything from the relationship between the sexes to the success or failure of political revolutions.

Very roughly, her theory goes like this: because the mother, representative of the female sex, is the one sole, unique and overwhelming presence in an infant's life, it is the female sex that comes to represent all the terrors, unpredictabilities, discomforts, magical powers, ultimate powers and deepest satisfactions felt in the shadowy and helpless consciousness of that infant. As the boy develops and struggles to separate himself from the mother, he will invest on an unconscious level *all* women with her awesome powers and feel that his aim in life as a man must be to keep women powerless for fear of their once-too-terrible dictatorship. It is a reaction at once real and neurotic, rather like the way Europeans flinch at any sign of German militarism or Jews scrutinize the smallest gentile action in the light of the Holocaust, but it is an undeserved punishment for the female sex who are ordinary human beings as well as mothers and yet are invested, willy-nilly, with hugely distorted infant memories. And because women are the infant-tenders, men are able to polarize their own personalities, taking for themselves all that seems rational, controlled, unemotional and practical as their difference and defence and leaving behind, projected upon the Other Sex, all the feelings that so disturbed them as helpless children.

Women, growing up, have also experienced the overwhelming sense of powerlessness, of blissful love and profound hatred, that their mothers have inevitably inspired and this earliest of emotions establishes the same grudge in them against the female sex. Female herself, she is divided against herself, finds it difficult to feel any solidarity with other women and lays down the first roots of masochism by lending herself to male punishment in order to punish, at one remove, her mother. To the girl, seeking to relieve the chaotic emotions aroused by mother, the father appears innocent of association with the inevitable griefs of infancy which are centred round the mother and so she seeks to loosen the ties with her own sex by establishing a worshipful, dependent stance towards men.

One of the many results of this early division between the sexes is that all women (symbols of all mothers) are the rubbish dumps for unacceptable feelings in both men and women. Instead of all individuals, when approaching maturity, having to resolve within themselves conflicting emotions and emerge as whole people, both men and women can reject whatever is disturbing upon the female sex and so avoid final maturity, which is the containment within of all parts of the personality and of the natural areas of 'masculinity' and 'femininity'.

There are other examinations of what it means to the adult woman to have been raised, often almost exclusively, by a woman or women. This is the chicken-and-egg situation par excellence. Women, labelled by society's laws and customs and its most profound unconscious as second-class citizens, are crippled by their experience. But they are the ones given the task of rearing the next generation who, not surprisingly, emerge equally crippled. And it is, naturally enough, the girl children who suffer most. Because women are female, they regard their sons as 'different', less knowable, more separate and therefore less manipulable. Boys are, on the whole, left free to find their own way to adulthood and, because of the masculine ethos, actively encouraged by mothers to be 'little men', meaning to be independent, adventurous and brave. The boys lose out to some extent through being given to understand that their emotions and admissions of vulnerability are not 'manly' but the essential tools necessary for building self-determination are willingly given.

The picture for little girls is very different. The mother, already hampered by a sense of her own inadequacies, feels herself on firmer ground with her daughter. She 'knows', after all, what women are and must be. Her own anxieties and insecurities she easily projects upon a girl, making her fearful of the outside world and instilling in her the agoraphobia that all women suffer to a greater or lesser extent. Because her own identity is not clear to her, because the price of the independence necessary to gain that identity seems too high, threatening as it does a future isolation and an essential 'unlovability' (and if a man does not love you, how will you live?), she does her best to train her daughter to be lovable. In tribal societies to this day it is the mother who forces painful circumcision of the clitoris and labia to make the girl acceptable to men. And the terms upon which, in our society and all previous societies, women can make themselves acceptable and beloved by men is to suppress all personal ambitions and needs in favour of the ambitions and needs of men.

Jean Baker Miller, in *Towards a New Psychology of Women,* defines the aims of dependent relationships, into which category fall parent–child relationships. The first, she says, might be called temporary inequality, in which the lesser party is socially defined as unequal and the concomitant aim on the part of the 'superior' or more knowledgeable is to bring the 'inferior' into full parity, to end the dependent relationship. It is the temporary inequality that mothers feel with their sons, though the irony is that they must educate not towards 'parity' but towards a domination. The second relationship teaches us how to enforce inequality but not how to make the journey from unequal to equal. This category includes all those defined by race, class, nationality or religion as for ever inferior to the 'teacher'. And those defined as inferior often teach their peers inferiority, having accepted that definition of themselves; mothers do exactly this with their daughters. For safety's sake and out of their own lack, they reproduce themselves.

Nor can mothers easily allow their daughter's sexuality to flourish without guilts. Given to understand, by generations of brainwashing, that a 'good' woman sublimates sex into motherhood, women, once married and particularly once mothers, cannot resolve two conflicting factors, their sexuality and that motherhood. Hints of it can be given a son, either in a mimicry of adult male–female ties or in the natural mild flirtations between sexes, but a daughter is disbarred. Mother presents herself as all-loving but sexless. There are added complications: the daughter's growing sexuality is often seen by the mother as a threat, another woman, a cuckoo-woman, in the nest and it is often also ignored and suppressed by the father, who feels conflict in the air and ducks the issue. More altruistically, sexuality in a girl is frequently interpreted by the mother as 'too active', an intrinsic part of a developing ego that spells only doom and loneliness for the child. For mothers, the signs of ego (identity) in a son prove her success in rearing a male. The same signs, in a daughter, set up miserable conflicts. How dare she be so selfish when the mother is sacrificial? How dare she risk such selfishness when the penalties are so harsh? Out of insecurity and a wish to protect, the mother does her assiduous best to crush her little woman's selfhood and turn her into one in a safe line of female nobodies.

And that is the terrible treachery between women, the first and consummate betrayal of female by female called mothering and daughterhood. We watch this woman, our mother, in her treadmill work, unpaid, unsung, and childishly believe that we, with luck and effort and virtue, will escape. Naively, we imagine ourselves different. We edge away from this slavish figure, down on her knees polishing the floor, always serving, standing as we eat, centre of our lives only while we ready ourselves to enter the wooden horse and storm the Troy of men. We learn to dislike our need of her, impatiently we drum our fingers as we wait for a freedom she has never known and we alone will gain. What is the first step to that freedom? Rejection of our mothers. Unworthy. This done, we turn smiling towards our father, towards the power-full three-ring-circus outside the hothouse home. Look, we say proudly. I am not like her, I am my father's daughter and absolutely different.

Then, to our amazement, the door to that outside world slams shut in our faces. The green baize door to above-stairs has closed and we are locked in the servants' hall below. A mistake has been made, do you hear me? Father, are you listening? Father, are you there? Our mothers come and stand behind us, touch our shoulders, gently pat our backs. I don't belong here, mother, I am not like you. She stands and strokes our hair until we turn and weep into her shoulder. We will never forgive her.

Betrayal is our father's sin, treachery our mother's. She knows everything and tells us nothing or, worse, she pretends. In the name of loyalty to her husband, our father, in the name of our own best interests, she will not breathe a word of what her life has been. Carefully she constructs a painting-by-numbers, helps our clumsy hands to fill the colours in. Fall in love – pink and red. Marry – shining white. Dear little babies – pink and blue. Happily ever after – silver and gold. Does she believe these are the proper colours? She blurred them herself, of course, got them wrong, but is she hoping that we will be luckier? When she comes round, years later, to cry over our kitchen table smeared with the food spat out by our own infants, sobbing of our father, what he has done, how she has lived, what she has put up with, what she really wanted to be, it is too late. Why didn't you tell me, mother? Why did you lie and lie? Because we are both women we do not blame our father and husband, distant old men puffing their pipes. We have long forgotten their betrayal. This woman could have saved us with a whiff of rebellion, the lift of an eyebrow, one laugh, one story, one truth. She withheld it all until we, too, were safely caged and then comes to share our imprisonment, down among the women. Two nobodies together.

'What do women want?' asked Freud. And answer comes there none because until women know they are somebody they cannot know what they want. Magically, then, they transfer their vague aspirations to men. Surely, if men are all-powerful, it is men who can give them what they want. Ever optimistic, they unite themselves in love and holy matrimony with the powerful male and wait, expectant, for him to wave a magic wand and fulfil the needs they have never themselves understood or articulated because they have never asked themselves, 'Who am I?' That, in the code of the mother, would be a selfish sin.

'O Oysters,' said the Carpenter,
'You've had a pleasant run!
Shall we be trotting home again?'
But answer came there none –
And this was scarcely odd, because
They'd eaten every one.

The 'eating' of women and their own conditioned wish to be absorbed into the flesh of others, to merge with their lovers and their children, has all sorts of interesting parallels in religious practices and even in national characteristics. Many of the old religions, the heresies like catharism and albigensianism that were stamped out by Christianity in the early Middle Ages, and also the Eastern religions until today, preach a fusion and an absorption into God which is anathema to the orthodox Christian in the West, who believes that God and man are divided by a fundamental abyss, what Kierkegaard called 'an infinite qualitative difference'. And there are whole countries – India is an outstanding example – which seem to have gone through a cultural and religious conditioning that bears startling similarities to women's conditioning and creates a whole people whose national psyche resembles the female psyche, with the same desire to sink individuality into something greater – a philosophy, a belief, a political cause, a God. Man sets up the altar and woman genuflects. Man proposes and woman prostrates herself.

Let me return to women as they are today: in whom the weaker super-ego creates more emotional, less competitive, more caring, more maternal beings largely dependent on others' approval. Though we all know (or are) women who sharply diverge from this generalization, we can surely agree that, at present, the description fits women as a whole far better than it fits men. And it would also seem to define women as the sex most literate in love, most able to love. Are we, then, the chosen ones, the new priestesses who will show mankind the way out of the wilderness and into the green and pleasant land of true love?

Not if we stay the way we are, we ain't. The sad fact is that for all women's apparent suitability for loving we are no better at it than men, and in some ways a good deal worse, if only because the world and her husband credit us with being experts in what we have hardly begun. If love was sacrifice, we would be acknowledged geniuses of love. If it were anticipation and fulfilment of the loved one's needs, we would be love goddesses. If love meant a fusion of the whole personality with the lover, we would be Venus herself. But love is none of these things and the something else it is, we are not good at and, at present, ill-equipped to give. The trouble is, we do not know ourselves, we do not recognize our inner vacuum and we call things by the wrong names.

Take sex, for instance. I have mentioned sex hardly at all so far, partly because it is mentioned a great deal practically everywhere else and partly because it seems to me that the bonding of animals and human beings for co-operation is paramount, love its pinnacle, and sexual activity a secondary method of strengthening and renewing these bonds. It is difficult to know what sex has meant to women in the past because their verdict on the subject was not usually voiced and, if voiced, not heard. But I suspect that whatever the verdict, it would have no relevance because they would not have been talking about sex at all. Like love, sex is a convenient umbrella word covering a multitude of different needs and motives and though the act itself is simple enough, the female half of the two-backed beast is rarely if ever there to get the same straightforward physical pleasure that comes to most men. Sex, in our case, has been for something else.

Listen to two women of my acquaintance talking. First, Jane:

Before I'd begun to think of myself as a person, I was just a woman. That meant I lived through men and on men and I had sex with them frequently and automatically. Then, slowly, through a longish programme of training and learning, I became financially independent. I was able to get my own place to live and buy for myself what I needed. Now I run my own life in every way and, do you know, I'm not sure I know what men are for any more. At exactly the same time as I began not to need them for my own security, whether physical or mental, I began not to need them for sex. Now, when a man makes a move towards bed, I almost always refuse. I just can't see the point.

And second; Susan:

I was always rather afraid of men, even though I had lots of boyfriends and no one would have guessed that inner fear. I was afraid of the power they represented, their aggression, their ridicule, their ability to make me feel unfeminine unless I conformed, unless I acted out the dolly bird with them. I suppose I hated them in a way, because I feared them. But none of that stopped me having sex and really enjoyable sex at that, lots of lovely orgasms. Then I met John, who was everything I had always wanted in a man – kind, gentle, intelligent and an egalitarian to his fingertips, he would never have dreamed of treating me as an inferior because he never thought of anyone that way. I fell in love with him and we live together now. But everything has gone horribly wrong because after a year or so, I just didn't want him sexually and now I never have an orgasm with him. It's very distressing for both of us and I feel humiliated beyond belief. Am I some kind of Neanderthal cow that actually needs bonking on the head and dragging into a cave to get my kicks?

Another woman I know caused amazement and gossip among her friends when she appeared to be taking on all the men in her office. Was she, after all, that famous female, your genuine nymphomaniac? I think not. The lady was ambitious but certain personality traits had made her unpopular. It would be quite wrong to say that she slept her way to the top. She didn't. The men she slept with did not help her in her job but they did stop hindering her. Quite clearly, her unconscious aim was to paralyse them, transform them from active enemies into passive neutrals and she succeeded in doing so.

Why would she not? Freud believed that aggression could not be eliminated but that it could be neutralized by activating all those forces which establish emotional bonds. Certainly all primates and some other animals use sex to appease the more dominant and aggressive among them, young animals of both sexes present themselves to placate older members just as adult females do to any threatening male. Appeasement through the offer of sex (which is quite often only accepted in a ritual mounting gesture without consummation) is surely as vital a part of the survival drive as reproduction, since an animal must guard its own life in order to reproduce. Nor is an unmistakably sexual form of appeasement confined to animals. In ancient Germania both men and women stuck their bared bottoms out of their front doors to propitiate the god Wotan, old Japanese protective amulets are carved in the form of bared buttocks, the Fulah women of Nigeria would present their backsides to strangers and bared buttocks are often shown on the outside of old fortresses and city gateways.

And after all appeasement of the male has been an historical imperative for women. It is the female sex that is vulnerable to male attack, the female sex that needs protection from the male and it is not surprising that women to this day use sex for many other reasons than simple satisfaction. If the orgasm is a late developer in women and still confined, apparently, to the few, it is no wonder, since pleasure was never the primeval aim. Jane lost her interest in sleeping with men when she learned how to provide for her own needs. Susan is a typical example of fear-bonding, very common and distressing to modern woman because it is often taken advantage of by aggressive men and often deplored by gentle egalitarian men who become cynical about women, saying that they give lip-service to male kindness but actually enjoy being treated badly. So it appears but it is not the whole truth. Susan is simply reacting as if she were an animal, which she is. Fear of men triggers a placatory reaction which is an ancient reflex, she is caught in an evolutionary trap which happens to be strong in her, probably because she has not yet won the battle for her own fully adult identity and self-respect. Perhaps the permissive society itself, with its increasing promiscuity, has the unconscious aim of neutralizing as much aggression as possible and strengthening the bonds that Freud believed were our only hope of avoiding war. The watchword is clear enough – make love, not war.

Nevertheless, an inner change in women which involves better, more aware, mothering of daughters should permit female sexuality to discard all the leftover elements of the past in favour of a straightforward interest in the sensations of sexual intercourse and pleasure in the partner. Passivity in general has many dangers that threaten both men and women but it is a traditional female trait so it is a particularly female threat. Aleister Crowley, a devotee of the black arts, used repeated sexual intercourse to send women into trances, during which time they were in his absolute control; the predominantly female worshippers of Dionysus arrived through sex at a state of possession in which they hurled themselves upon wild animals and tore them to pieces 'for the joy of the raw feast'; Mesmer's female clients submitted to his control in sexual passivity and Professor Dinnerstein notes that the particular passivity of masochism in women gives them far less freedom in love than their counterparts.

As long as women remain passive in sex, they distort it, making it a primary instead of a secondary bonding force. The trance-like, rather than the active sexual state, is a kind of brainwashing (see Chapter 5) in which the reasoning faculties lose control. When women 'fall in love' in such a state, that love is of their own creation and answers their own needs. It is, in the widest sense, self-centred because it almost entirely disregards the other human being involved as a separate, distinct person. An awful unity is achieved, of a kind much praised for its convincing façade, in which the man and the woman 'become one'. But all this means, in reality, is that each partner (and especially the female partner) imprints herself with the male in as mechanistic a way as Lorenz's ducklings. It is impossible to apprehend who he really is, what he really needs, or to feel any detached joy in his existence, and so true love is impossible. I have always felt uneasy about feminist claims that men have denied women their sexuality and that male fears of women's rampant insatiability lie at the root of the myth that women are not as much in need of sex as men. They may be right but they cannot be entirely right. If sex were really the basic and overwhelmingly powerful drive we are told it is, then surely no amount of conditioning would have succeeded in turning women into the relatively asexual beings some of them certainly were and are. But if sex were, after all, just another way of strengthening the bonds of the co-operation so essential to social life or even a method of avoiding the aggression that might threaten social life, then it would hardly be surprising that women, who need to invoke co-operation and avoid aggression far more than men, have used sex for these purposes more often and much longer than men.

In the future, with more financial independence and outside opportunities for women and the kind of mothering that allows girls enough identity to make their sexuality an expression of themselves rather than a manipulative device for survival, plus secure mothers who have resolved their own conflicts between Virgin Mary Mother and Mary Magdalene and so do not pass on to their daughters the idea that sex is dirty, then, perhaps, at last women will be able to experience sex as purely pleasurable and purely pleasure-giving.

When we talk of love, as opposed to sex, we cannot countenance any thought of manipulation. To use love in such a way is to negate its existence. However, all of us are guilty, if that is the right word for what we *must* do, of unconscious manipulation to assuage deep needs. Woman's lack of a super-ego, her dependence upon the approval of others and her conditioning to sublimate her own desires in nurturing others is not a formula geared to give the sort of love to another human being that answers his/her needs rather than the woman's own. Unresolved desires, suppressed in the individual, are then projected upon the other so that though we may feel as if we sacrifice our lives, as women, in fulfilling our husbands' and our children's needs, in fact we may be doing nothing of the sort. Their needs are not ours (or, in the case of children, not yet). But so literally are we wrapped up, neurotically, in ourselves that their separateness, their individual needs, are not apparent. Thus is created that archetypally pitiful female – the woman martyr who has done everything for her lover/husband/children (worked her fingers to the bone, given the best years of her life) and yet is abandoned, yet is deserted, yet is unloved. The edicts of society being what they are, the woman is constantly reaffirmed in her sacrifice and constantly promised that it will bring her love. The truth is otherwise. Between one flesh, the Christian idea of love and marriage, there is no true love because the idea itself is false. For two to become as one is for each of the two to become useless to the other and women, until now, have done their best and seen it as their duty to merge. The price of human consciousness is an awareness of individuality and the consolation is the love that recognizes that individuality and holds out a loving hand over that separateness.

Fusion, that peculiarly feminine form of love, is a kind of obscenity, a spiritual parasitism. It contributes nothing and increases the problems that exist. If a woman sees everything through her husband's eyes, she offers him no different viewpoint to balance his own, if she lives through him she can provide no separate experience for his use, by his side there is no individual human being who has faced the same battles in the outside world as he has but only a grown-up child who clings to him, hoping that he will somehow manage for both of them, live for both of them. That kind of love, so often called loyalty or self-sacrifice or even 'letting the man wear the pants', I call the old woman of the sea syndrome. Carry me, I don't want to get my feet wet.

It is men's fault, if such a word adequately covers the patriarchal ethos that has kept women in subjugation and turned so many of us into burdensome children, and our flawed love is their penalty. But now, at last, the very needs of our planet are beginning to present the conditions for change. As woman's world widens from a small domestic centre to take in the complexities of the outside world, as she is enabled to make her way in that outside world without special protection or special penalties, as her inner psyche begins to change in response to these outer changes and a strong sense of her own identity emerges along with enough confidence for the needs of that identity to be voiced and assuaged, so will she begin to be able to love freely, choose freely and offer her detached, hard-won wisdom to a beloved man. Until now, women have not been mistresses enough of themselves even to choose a man for himself, for his own especial virtues and idiosyncrasies. For generations forced into marriages of convenience, we are still forced by our unfulfilled needs and, unable to do anything about them ourselves, turn to men for our answers. I pick a rich man to solve my survival problems. You find a famous man to give you an ego at one remove. She falls for a helpless man to use up her unused power drives. Her sister is hooked by a wife-beater who fills her with primeval terror or expresses her own aggression or makes her feel a martyr – anything as long as it is her need and not his. Many women settle for a weak and kindly man whom they treat as a son, hoping that all will go well enough if only they can keep him out of trouble, away from drink and the lure of other women. Nanny wife and naughty boy.

It is a bitter irony for men that their insistence on woman's inferiority, their refusal to grant her a place in the sun, has robbed them of the only chance they have to love and be loved properly. They cannot love women because they have made women unequal to themselves and forced them, therefore, into all the unloving patterns of inequality. And women cannot love them because the inferior do not properly love their masters, they only prostrate (or prostitute) themselves, or live vicariously through them.

But all is not lost – there is a silver lining to the female cloud of oppression. Our whole world now stands in dire need of people with exactly the sort of inner psychic structure women have, perforce; those traits Freud cited as proof of a kind of failure – less competitive, less aggressive, more dependent on the approval of others, less strongly influenced by abstract codes of behaviour, more loving, more maternal. He added 'more emotional' to his list of feminine characteristics because even the master was a man and failed to see that while women may appear more emotional (they have hysterics, they weep, they have the vapours) men have their full quota of emotions too, only theirs are respectable and called other names, like war. If women can somehow manage to become autonomous people with good healthy egos and still retain all the traits that were formed by subjugation, that will be the triumph for them and for humanity.

In terms of mothering, bringing up daughters, this means a radical change in the parental structure. First: both men and women must become equally responsible for bringing up children. This does not mean that within each individual family a particular father or a mother cannot take more or less responsibility; only that children need to see both sexes as possible child-rearers so that neither sex can possibly be considered as 'the other', to become the dump for all unwanted, disturbing and unresolved emotions. Second: the woman must have equal status in society and equal opportunities to make her own living, so that her survival needs are within her own control. Thirdly, the mother must have equal status within the family so that if she happens to be the one who mainly cares for the infants, she cannot be seen to ally herself with the children against the father but with adults in an outside world towards which she is ushering her children. When the father no longer embodies any particular authority or reflection of the status quo by virtue of his sex alone, then the whole Freudian structure of penis envy and Oedipal struggle may fall, at least in its most static form. Who knows what children will make of the business of childhood when they are faced, for the first time in history, with uniquely individual parents who can only be divided into sexes by the rough measure of genitalia?

The development of an ego, a centre, in women is not necessary just so they may love and be loved truly. Nor is it only something they must struggle towards for their own individual fulfilment. There is a far more vital reason that turns the search and the struggle into an absolute duty to the human race and its survival. Until today, women have been the submerged half of humanity and have been weakened by that submergence, rendered passive and ego-less, forced to find what identity they could through a fusion with men's identities, men's egos. In that fusion, they have condoned what should not have been condoned and nourished monsters that could have been left to starve. But if they do not change as they gain equality and power in the world, if they rush on to the stage quaking with emotion and longing still for something before which they may kneel, oh what a spectre looms, what a regiment of monstrously amenable women will swell the ranks of evil, what dead weights will be set against reason.

Let me preach the parable of Susan Atkins, ex-Charlie Manson groupie, or rather, let her preach it. From memories of her childhood:

People stretched and turned to see the tiny figure walking nervously down the aisle, the one who had received the greatest number of gold stars for her Sunday School lessons. I was not quite three years old on that Sunday morning in 1951 ... I glanced swiftly up at the man on the cross. I hoped I had pleased him somehow. He loved little children and I desperately wanted him to love me too ...

Grown-up Susan met Al. 'I had faith in Al. I knew he could take care of me. He was big, beautiful – and mysterious. I was in love with him and with the mystery of him. Even if he wasn't precise about what was ahead, I still trusted him.' Her big, beautiful, mysterious Al was an ex-con, on the run from his parole agent. In a stolen car with a rifle in the back. Susan and Al set out for a 'big heist'. Al told her that after this robbery, he would settle down and marry her. 'My faith in him', said Susan, 'was so great that I believed him.' Both of them ended in jail.

Then Susan met Charlie Manson. 'All your roots are cut,' said Charlie. 'You are freed from your families and all their old hangups. You are cut loose into the now. You are free. And because we are free, we can become one. The Bible says we must die to self and that's exactly true. We must die to self so that we can be at one with all people. That is love.' Charlie washed Susan's feet. 'No, Charlie,' said Susan, 'you can't do that. I'm not worth it.' 'Susan,' said Charlie, 'you are perfect. You are one with God. We're all one in him. I must wash your feet. I must show the way.' Susan says, 'All consciousness and awareness of my individual self slipped away. I had no idea who I was – only that I was in total oneness with everyone ... in the whole world.'

Charlie asked Susan to go and 'get' Gary Hinman and she went and watched him murdered. Charlie asked Susan to 'get' the La Biancas and everyone at the Polanski house and she went and 'got' them. To the weeping Sharon Tate, eight months pregnant, she said, 'Look, bitch, I don't care if you're going to have a baby. You'd better be ready. You're going to die.' Then she dipped a towel in the murdered woman's blood and wrote 'Pig' on the front door.

Why? Because Charlie was God. 'Charlie was there alone. He was dressed in a long white robe. I immediately knew that he might be God himself; if not, he was close to him.' Susan told her cellmate of how Charlie would put himself on a cross and one of the girls would kneel at its foot while he moaned as if he were being crucified.

Susan was condemned to death and reprieved by the ending of the death penalty. In her cell she had a vision. 'The whitest, most brilliant light I had ever seen poured over me ... there was only light. And in the centre of the flood of brightness was an even brighter light. Vaguely, there was the form of a man. I knew it was Jesus.'

And now little Susan Atkins is a dedicated Christian who speaks with tongues. To Jesus she has dedicated a book describing the long and arduous trek from Jesus Manson to Jesus Jesus. Now she is bringing the word of the Lord to the sad, defeated women at the Californian Institute for Women. To Cathy, homosexual and drug addict, she says that lesbianism is a sin. 'But it can be forgiven and you can be changed, stopped from sinning, if you want to. Jesus forgives you. He loves you.' 'And,' concludes Susan triumphantly, 'when she was released from prison, an entirely different person walked out the front gate, delivered from one of the most blatant sins found in a women's prison.'

Susan Atkins's book is entitled *Child of Satan, Child of God*. The operative word is neither Satan nor God but Child. Poor, ghastly Susan is set apart from a vast army of her sisters only by the fact that the man she chose to love and obey asked her to murder for him rather than merely run his household or be his company wife. It has been widely assumed that Charlie Manson brainwashed his women because brainwashing is a convenient and acceptable explanation for otherwise inexplicable behaviour. How else could we bear the image of the pretty long-haired Manson girls, who look so like ourselves or our daughters, soaked in the blood of their terrified victims? Obviously, they were in the thrall of a male fiend, their heads scrambled by his wicked words, as much puppets on his strings as any Manchurian Candidate. So that solves the Atkins–Krenwinkle–Squeaky Fromm–Van Houten–Kasabian problem and all we need do is bury it and walk away.

But there is another and far more frightening explanation for the Manson girls and that lies in their profound *resemblance* to many other women. Vincent Bugliosi remarked:

There was a little girl quality to them, as if they hadn't aged but had been retarded at a certain stage in their childhood. Each was, in her own way, a pretty girl. But there was a sameness about them that was much stronger than their individuality ... same expressions, same patterned responses, same tone of voice, same lack of distinct personality. The realization came with a shock – they reminded me less of human beings than of Barbie Dolls.

That is a comment on an external resemblance but it goes deeper than the skin. It goes so deep that it reveals ways in which all womankind is like the Manson women. The Colonel's lady and Judy O'Grady, goes the old saw, are sisters under the skin and in one crucial way we are all sisters of Atkins and Krenwinkle, Eva Braun, Frau Stangl. Alan Scheflin and Edward Opton, in *The Mind Manipulators*, analyse the Manson women: 'They all felt alone and afraid in the world around them. They did not have clear identities in search of a place. Rather, they searched for a place to obtain an identity.' But in all Scheflin and Opton's analyses, both of people and manipulative techniques, right through to their conclusions on resisting manipulations of the mind, 'The real enemy lies within ourselves, in the human desire to dominate and the willingness to submit,' and, 'By valuing our own individuality, that ineffable uniqueness of each person's existence, we will learn to resist those who seek to devalue us all' – they never actually crystallize one simple fact. It is not all human beings but one sex in particular that is conditioned into submissiveness, conditioned out of individuality, refused a crucial identity and that sex is, of course, female. No wonder the groupies of this world are women. Charlie Manson may have brainwashed his girls to some extent but they were well on the way when he met them – because they were female.

Once upon a time, that inner vacuum in women posed no threat and was extremely useful to those who had power, men. It served their ends, whether they were ordinary men-in-the-street whose wives obeyed them as heads of the household or dictators who needed sex and comfort after a day spent ordering torture and death. But today, as women begin the long haul to equality and men themselves see the dawning need for female participation in coping with the world's problems, they may find they have, indeed, created a horde of Frankenstein's Brides. More than fifty years ago, English Labour politicians argued against giving women the vote on the grounds that they were too impressionable, too easily swayed by a well-cut suit or a handsome face. The fact is they were probably right, but what they never perceived was that they themselves had forced women into this mould from childhood. If you bind the feet of infant girls and break the growing bones, you cannot complain, later, that women are no good at walking.

The recent literature on mind manipulation is extensive. Throughout history, the methods by which men condition, brainwash, tamper with and otherwise use the brain for power ends have obvious similarities, many of which are explored in Chapter 5. There are additional ones. The Chinese methods of thought reform, adopted by policy-makers for certain American prisons, include: physically removing prisoners to areas sufficiently isolated effectively to break or seriously weaken close emotional ties, convincing prisoners that they can trust no one, treating those who are willing to collaborate in far more lenient ways than those who are not, punishing those who show unco-operative attitudes, rewarding submission and subservience with a lifting of pressure and acceptance as human beings and providing social and emotional supports which reinforce 'proper' attitudes. Other processes picked out by experts on brainwashing include *identification*: people tend very strongly to identify themselves with and model themselves on others. If the only other person one sees is an inquisitor, one identifies with him. So one of the first steps is the deliberate breaking down of identity, by stripping away the symbols of individuality, including status and name.

It seems to me no exaggeration to glimpse within these classic techniques something of what has been done to women, from force of habit, over the generations, with a few more recent refinements. For the past seventy years or so women have been isolated in marriage, often quite literally alone, day after day, in an empty house. Often the wife has had to uproot herself from family and friends to follow her husband to strange places and strange lands. Many men give their wives to understand that they should trust only their lord and master and have divided them off with jealousies and rivalries from their own sex, leaving the woman to identify only with her 'inquisitor' himself. Her very name is taken away from her as part of the marital sacrament and as she becomes submissive and subservient, she, too, will be rewarded, given 'the social and emotional supports which reinforce the attitudes'.

From all this emerges an individual without individuality, a Barbie Doll who, if she does not actually look very similar to other women, will do her best to conform to a stereotype by masking her features with cosmetics and concealing her hair under a fashionable helmet. The only part of the brain-washing process that women do not have to undergo is the breaking down of their identity – that was already, lovingly, accomplished in childhood. And there the processed woman is, physically full-grown but curiously retarded, little-girlish, soft clay to be moulded by any outside influence, waiting for a man (or a cause) who will make her complete by allowing her to partake of his ego and further his purposes. If he is a pimp, she will prostitute herself for him; if he batters her, she will put up with it; if he is religious, so is she; if he votes Tory, so will she.

So the struggle of women today to construct an identity and form a self from selflessness is a vital struggle that should be supported by all people of goodwill who want to see, in the future, no man abetted in his own corruption and no woman a dangerous puppet, easily manipulated, a passive passenger on any political or mystical bandwagon that promises to fill the vacuum inside.

EIGHT

The Logic

'Tell me where is fancy bred,
Or in the heart or in the head?'

No good is done the cause of love or of humanity at large if
women develop their egos and continue to feel that emotion is
their particular and sacred gift. Traditionally, we have all
agreed that the heart is where fancy is bred because we
prefer to think of ourselves as mysterious rather than explic-
able, our emotions irrational rather than predictable, and we
happily enshrine love as the most mysterious of all the
emotions, an ineffable spirit that descends upon us from the
heavens at random and without possibility of control by anything so mechanistic as the head. We revel in love's uncon-
trollability, we expect its acceptance as such by our fellow
men, we fight any encroachment of reason upon its chaos
because as long as love is believed to stem from the heart it is
an escape from reason that is sanctioned by society, a holy
possession to be admired, envied or pitied by others but
never to be accounted the lover's responsibility. Like drunk-
enness, love allows us permission to do what we want.

Which is odd because today we understand almost everything about the functioning of the heart and, for that
matter, those medieval seats of love, the stomach and the
bowels. It is the brain that is the twentieth-century mystery,
that heavy wrinkled organ that most clearly divides us from
the rest of the animal kingdom. Perhaps that is the clue –
throughout history we have stoutly fought any hint, any
idea, that seems to link us, however tenuously, with animals.
They behave because they must, we behave because we will,
or so we think. The brain that separates us, the consciousness
that plagues us so, the 'love' we do not share with animals,
must be seen to have no roots in animal life, otherwise there
is no justification for the torments we suffer and the inno-

cently calm, instinctive lives they lead. Bitterly we envy them and so we must invent a higher purpose for ourselves, otherwise what is all the fuss about?

And yet when it suits us we lay claim to the reasoning faculties as if we had never, in the whirl of love, denied them. Though we wish to retain the escape-hatch of the heart, we reckon our other superiorities in terms of the head and whenever we want to point out the inferiority of another human being, we call them dumb, thick, stupid, weak in the head.

The clearest example of this is the way in which men, the dominant sex, call themselves the reasoning sex, cool, rational, mathematical, logical, and label women intuitive creatures, slaves to the emotions, easily swayed, irrational, innumerate, illogical. Women, they say, do not reason, women feel. Men proceed by outer realities, women by inner upheavals and that is why women are designated the loving sex. In this context, love is a childish emotion, a consolation prize awarded underlings to keep their minds off dangerous discontent and enable men falsely to praise them, pretend to envy them and, meanwhile, rule the world.

Women protest that in that world the feminine intuitive and subjective powers are rendered null and void. They complain that if they wish to participate in the masculine system they must submit to masculinization, give up their hearts in favour of the cold hard head and so become rational pseudo-males, that is to say men in skirts, that is to say second-class men. This is the fear of a kind of feminism. Scornfully, these feminists analyse the male judgment of a certain woman – 'She thinks like a man' – and translate it: 'This female has somehow overcome her gender disability and seems to be able to use her neo-cortex in rational decision-making.' Therefore, they jeer, she may be accounted an honorary homo sapiens. The male remark 'That's just like a woman' they translate as 'This female manifests the characteristic cerebral defects of the XX chromosomal behaviour determinants. She is largely restricted to decision-making via limbic/hypothalamic/neuronal pathways with little evidence of neocortical influences and is more accurately classified as Homo Emotionalis or Homo Gonadis.' Their translation is right but overtly defensive. It has no need to be.

The neo-cortex is the newest portion of the brain in evolutionary terms. The limbic system is the old or paleocortex governing emotion and the functions and behaviour of humans that are shared by 'lower' species. The hypothalamic is the oldest or 'lizard' brain governing automatic and 'vegetable' functions regulating hormones and reflex action. To put it crudely, we share the lizard brain with lizards, the paleocortex with mammals and only the new brain, the neo-cortex, is completely human in the sense that it and it alone provides those attributes that set us well apart from even the highest primates – memory, language, abstraction, logic, rationality and all the many other offcuts of consciousness. So when these feminists persist in denigrating the 'male' logic and attributing emotion unsullied by logic to women they are in fact, if not in intent, placing women on a par with the primates and lower on the evolutionary ladder than the opposite sex.

Indeed, those who believe that woman is the emotional sex – in other words, Queen of the hypothalamus or 'old brain' – must contend with recent theories that this old brain will be the death of us unless we manage to control it with reason. Arthur Koestler, for instance, points out that neurophysiological evidence suggests an actual biological basis for the separation of these 'male' and 'female' territories of the brain, not that he designates them as such. The split between reason and emotion, he thinks, has its origin in the neuroanatomy of the brain. Due to evolutionary development, there is insufficient co-ordination between the hypothalamus, the older, more primitive 'female' brain structure, and the neo-cortex, the relatively recent 'male' superstructure involved in intellectual functions. Koestler speculates as to the impending genosuicidal extinction of the human species because of the lack of integration between these structures. If you like, a kind of physical blueprint of the old battle of the sexes.

Others believe that a separation of the intuitive holistic

'feminine' functions and the analytic logical 'masculine' functions of the brain shows itself in terms of left-right hemispherical specializations. Certainly this view is echoed in many philosophies, from Freud's conscious and unconscious and Jung's masculine and feminine principles to the Eastern yin and yang, a universal dichotomy that may have its physical basis in the cerebral anatomy. Some feminists feel that the suppression of what were originally meant to be complementary components (anima and animus) has prevented each sex from becoming fully human. They are, of course, correct in their underlying premise that neither sex has a monopoly on thought or emotion but the conclusion – that the 'feminine' or emotional aspect is actually the prerogative of women and so has been ignored and refused the status needed to redress the balance – seems at best misguided and at worst reveals a curious refusal to confront reality.

Sue Cox, American author of *Feminine Psychology: The Emerging Self*, says, 'Academic feminists wish to redefine psychology by giving feelings and intuition an equal status with thinking for both women and men,' and some of these academics run Women's Studies courses in American universities aimed at doing just this. They too, believe that the emotions are largely women's province, have been rejected by men in favour of more objective thought processes and deserve upgrading. They are not alone in their belief. Recently, the English feminist magazine *Spare Rib* published an interview with an avowed feminist who had just returned from an Indian ashram. She described the process of 'going orange', donning the orange robes that signify a follower of the enlightened master Bhagwan Shree Rajneesh, a path she says many other feminists are taking. The Bhagwan, we are told, points out that it is

the logical thinking, organized, rational male mind which prevents one from experiencing oneself and one's physical being, sensations and feelings. My mind, I realize, is conditioned totally, 99 per cent by what you could call a sort of patriarchal mind, a desire to be logical, realistic, materialistic. Now I see that trying to work out women's problems through the male mind is destructive and useless. In fact, to work out any problem through the mind is useless because it doesn't really touch your own bodies or sensations.

There we have it, the barmy acceptance by many women and even some militant feminists that the qualities men have described as 'female' through the centuries are essentially correct and only need dusting off and polishing up to take their rightful place in a deprived society. Men lay claim to rational thought and their claims are believed by women. Men say women are emotional and their judgment is believed by women. So all that women have to do is claim equal rights for feminine emotion (or, in the case of Bhagwan followers, exalt emotion's superiority) and all in women's world will be well. The fact that the Bhagwan's formula (preached by many of the holy men of India) has kept India herself among the most poverty-stricken, downtrodden and manipulable populations of the world is not, apparently, something that deters the affluent Western sister in search of herself.

What all this amounts to is a brainwashing campaign by men of women and women of themselves upon a truly staggering scale. They have paid the piper and women are still dancing to their tune. The only change is that women are now pretending the tune is their own. The fact is that any examination, however cursory, of male history, male actions or male institutions immediately reveals one glaring truth: the amount of logic, rationality, objectivity or even common sense to be found there could be stood on the end of a pin. The history of the whole human race, male and female, is a history stemming from the mammal brain, cloudy with superstition, credulity and emotion, while the neo-cortex lies like virgin land, unexplored, its switchboard to reason barely connected, its potential untapped. Men do not need to develop their emotional faculties, they are already hideously overdeveloped. Women do not need to concentrate any effort at all on giving emotion status, it is the overspill of emotion that has kept them in chains until now. Both sexes share one overwhelming necessity – to begin to use what is still virgin territory, the reasoning function of the neo-cortex.

A bird's-eye view of mankind's reasoning achievements shows them dotted haphazardly here and there through the centuries like distant stars, gleaming fitfully, falling and dying. Whatever small body of knowledge based on logic has been amassed in one era has either been eliminated later by the emotions of aggression, ambition and fear or simply fallen into disuse and been forgotten in yet another swing of the pendulum of emotional barbarism. Until the invention of printing, a few laboriously hand-written books contained the sum total of men's thoughts and these were easily destroyed, leaving the thoughts themselves to surface perhaps two thousand years later. And when knowledge survived it was frequently either ignored out of men's preference for fantasy or deliberately suppressed to allow that fantasy to flourish.

A brief summary of the rational, logical, unemotional, objective male mind at work through the centuries: Three and a half thousand years ago an Egyptian scribe copied out the solutions to simple equations and the devices for handling fractions and finding areas and volumes but he was forbidden to give general rules by other men who called themselves priests. Two thousand three hundred years ago Anaxagoras, Greek scientist and rationalist, was accused of impiety and atheism and brought to trial, the first of a long line of scientists to be thus persecuted. In about 600 BC the Greek philosopher Thales became the first man on record to explain the universe without resort to gods or demons but millions today still prefer the supernatural god-made view. A little later, Xenophanes expounded the fact that the physical characteristics of the earth had changed with time but his theory was ignored for twenty-three centuries. Alcmaeon, Greek physician, was the first known individual to have conducted dissections of the human body but that practice was soon banned as sacrilegious. Empedocles glimpsed the pattern of evolution two thousand years before Darwin; Philolaus speculated on the earth's movement through space and Aristarchus that the earth revolved about the sun two thousand years before Copernicus, who himself was persecuted.

Such knowledge does not get lost as you and I might lose a

hat in a sudden tug of wind. Men's eyes are deliberately blinded to it by emotion. Sometimes such knowledge is not so much ignored as carefully buried six feet under because some mystic cult has proclaimed that knowledge anathema. Since time began, the vast majority of our human race has chosen to explain the mysterious with a mystery, a religion, rather than attempting to use the faculties of reason. Religion, any religion, is the apotheosis of unreason, whether the devotee worships a marmoset for embodying the spirit of his grandfather, prostrates himself before an image of Jesus's face on the sole of a shoe (as happened in 1978 in Quebec) or sits with a golden hat on his head and calls himself infallible. And there has never been a society without religion, most of them dreamed up by and for the benefit of the male sex.

True to their emotional source, the religious have always developed nervous spasms at the very hint of the use of the neo-cortex. Faith is all and faith has its seat in the limbic system, the mammalian brain, with large parts of the ritualistic and hierarchical reptile brain added to it. Throughout history, Reason has sent out guerilla forces from the neo-cortex, exploding sticks of facts under the long caravanserai of limbic unreason but each breach of man's ignorance was quickly repaired and its executors captured, harried, tortured and murdered.

Under unreasoning Christianity, as with its foreign counterparts, the war has gone on. Reason used women as partisans, pointing out that if human beings have souls and women are human beings, then women have souls. Bishops and churchmen across a continent, thrown into disarray, set up conferences to prove that this could not be so and their unreason flourishes to this day, since women are still considered unfit for priesthood among most Protestants and all Catholics. The Italian Copernicus reasoned that the earth revolved around the sun and that it revolved along with other planets. The implication was clear. This earth, centre of God's work, his White House, his Buckingham Palace, home of his masterpiece, Man, was just another orb, subordinate, a fringe entity, its very mass under the control of the moon. Unreason refused Copernicus's facts, his findings were not published until the year of his death and his book banned by the Catholic Church until 1835. Years later, Galileo put his seal on Copernicus's discovery, was hauled up before the Inquisition on charges of heresy, and forced to recant. He was refused burial in consecrated ground; his book, too, was banned by the Church until 1835. *Eppur si muove.* Against all the battalions of unreason, these two men had started a scientific (and a neo-cortical) revolution.

Six decades before Charles Darwin, James Hutton advanced the first principles of geology and natural selection and met with strong resistance from an Establishment that preferred the biblical account of creation. When Darwin concluded that men were descended from apes, all hell broke loose. Queen Victoria refused him honours, the great British Prime Ministers William Gladstone and Benjamin Disraeli opposed him – 'I,' said Disraeli, 'am on the side of the angels.' Darwin's contemporary, Sir James Simpson, was the first man to use anaesthesia in childbirth and caused an outcry because he threatened one of unreason's most cherished tenets – that women should bring forth children in anguish to fulfil the curse of Eve.

Every time one man has used his logic and reason, a hundred thousand other men have abused him for so doing, in the name and in the grip of emotion. The long struggle is epitomized in Mary Shelley's nineteenth-century novel *Frankenstein,* in which her scientist Count, driven by what is supposed to be his evil lust for more and more knowledge, produces the ultimate blasphemy, life itself. Is Frankenstein's Monster truly monstrous or only a first miraculous experiment immediately persecuted, hounded and transformed into a monster by this persecution? Are there some things too sacred, too dangerous, too mysterious for man to probe or must he follow wherever his increasing skills lead him? The argument is ever more furious and more relevant as we begin to understand the very source of life itself but the voice of unreason is louder than ever before, a Cassandra for ever predicting disaster and catastrophe as a punishment for what it sees as man's audacity rather than man's destiny, given his particular physical equipment. Since the world's first test-tube baby was born the Church has denounced the process, and already an American woman's laboratory-fertilized egg has been destroyed by a Catholic doctor.

Over the generations, many people have fought furiously against any hint that mankind could learn to control his fate or his reproductive faculties. To them the very idea is blasphemous. Curiously, though, they have never objected to wars as a form of population control, particularly wars of total unreason. The Crusades cost millions of lives, decimated three generations and were fought in the name of two Gods – Jesus and Mahomet. Perhaps well over nine million women lost their lives in the European witch hunts in the fight against the anti-God, Satan, as did thousands of souls in the Inquisition. In our own time the Lebanon has been torn apart in a religious war, the dictator Idi Amin has murdered an estimated 500,000 members of Christian tribes in his Moslem Uganda, Northern Ireland is charred and pitted with a religious battle and the whole of the Middle East remains a powder keg, threatening us all, because one race believes in its inalienable right, through religion, to territory that others believe is theirs.

Unreason, in 1979, is alive and well and living anywhere you care to name and never has it threatened us more. But just at this time, as women, a whole half of the human race, arise to demand their place in the sun, they are in grave danger of proclaiming themselves peculiarly gifted apostles of unreason, prophetesses come to show these logical men the error of their ways.

Many women ascribe the evils of this century – pollution, the arms race, Third World poverty, the spoliation of wars, the extinction of other species, a spiralling crime rate, drugs, delinquency and exploitation in general – to men's meddling. And there is a supreme illogicality here. These are the men women also accept as being the reasonable, unemotional sex who have erred only in giving very low status to that wonder of women's lives, emotion. But what has pollution, war, crime, drug addiction or the decimation of animals to do with logic? Each is a product of uncontrolled emotions: competitiveness, ambition, chauvinism, greed, aggression, blind selfishness, misery, jealousy, resentment. Oddly, feminists often talk in the same breath of men's insistence on the merits of reason and their own dislike of men's appalling sins. The two cannot logically co-exist and yet, so brainwashed are such women, so resigned to men's estimate of themselves, that they do not see the contradiction. Worse, they vaunt their own emotional approach to life as if it were something unique in the world, a truly new contribution by women, failing utterly to see that, when they talk with pride even about so small an instance as feminine intuition, they are labelling as mysterious feeling what is in fact a useful process emanating from logic and the reasoning faculties. Intuition is, after all, the vague umbrella title given to acute observation of a myriad small signs and the perfectly logical conclusions to be drawn therefrom. And, confident of their special emotional powers, they retire into corners to play the tarot cards or throw yarrow sticks or do the *I Ching*, counting these games a part of women's wisdom that has been 'negated' by cool masculine minds and must now be given its proper importance in the halls of academe. Men it was, of course, who invented the tarot pack, the yarrow sticks and wrote the *I Ching*.

Sadly, this acceptance of male logical powers reveals only the true depths of women's separation from the life of the world. Huddled, alone in our houses, we take for granted that men are correct in their assessment of masculine intellectuality, though one look at a newspaper, one glimpse of the Houses of Parliament in session, the White House at work, the Bundestag operating could show us in seconds the ludicrousness of such an assessment. Recently, in England, debates in the House of Commons have been broadcast and shock waves spread through voters from Land's End to John o' Groat's. Mercy on us, these men act like children, and badly behaved ones at that.

It has not, apparently, occurred to some women that they, too, possess a neo-cortex, that the development of that wrinkled upper brain was not evolved by men alone, that it took the combined necessities of humankind to grow that bulge behind the neck that signals reason. In fact, this failure to claim an equal neurological inheritance is hardly surprising. Not only have women been denied much chance to express our rational faculties but generations of male propaganda praising our warm hearts and pretty little ways may be to blame for the widespread female conspiracy to conceal the former and exaggerate the latter. It is a wonder that intelligence was not bred out of women long ago and it is a testimony to the toughness of submerged femininity that, given at last the chance to practise rationality, young women enrolling in ever increasing numbers at universities are taking more and better degrees than men.

Certainly, anthropologists have succeeded in conveying the strong impression that it was only due to male concerns and activities that the human race ever stood up on its hind legs, grew its large brain and became a social being. *Time* magazine summed up the general male-centred view in a long article on homo habilis published in 1978.

The process of natural selection favored those of his genus who could stand up; an erect position enabled them to see over the tall grass to spot and hunt their prey . . . Homo habilis began to make tools and to hunt. Both actions accelerated his evolution. Tool-making, which required reasoning and more complex neurological hookups, gave a survival advantage to the creatures with the biggest brains. That led to an increase in brain size. Hunting, with its emphasis on outwitting animals that were either faster, stronger or fiercer than the hominids that hunted them, also stimulated rapid brain growth. In addition . . . it placed a premium on co-operation, strengthening the bond between members of the group and starting man on the road toward developing language.

Clearly, *Time* believes that only male necessities contributed to evolutionary change. The other half of the race was apparently a dead weight, so many rag dolls who had somehow to be forced to stand upright and be moulded into human beings by the male hunters and weapon-makers. Like the names and lineage of women that are submerged and forgotten in marriage and male family trees, the evolutionary pressures upon women – though vitally concerned with the reproduction of the race – are lost in androcentricity. And yet the few facts available speak as loudly for the possibility that it was women who invented or discovered many of the most reasonable, logical and beneficial things, from medicine and pottery to animal husbandry and agriculture itself. It is not outside the bounds of possibility that women, who needed to communicate with their children at least as badly as men to their hunting band, also did their share in inventing language.

Elaine Morgan points out the absurdities of an androcentricity that appears to view the development of men and women as a kind of apartheid or worse – separate but unequal. Her belief that it was the female hominids who first stood up because they discovered that to retreat into sea and lakes was their best method of protecting themselves and their infants and they had literally to keep their heads above water, makes at least as much sense. Tool-making is not confined to making hunting weapons either – hominids were also gatherers and you need tools to dig out edible roots as badly as you need them to kill animals. If hunting was the activity that created the social being, it is inconceivable that females did not, under the same pressures of survival for themselves and their offspring, realize the necessity of grouping with other females.

We, the women of the West, are slowly emerging to take over some of the running of our late-twentieth-century society and we should lay claim to our natural inheritance, that intricate switchboard that constitutes the neo-cortex. This is our real inner space and not the mammal brain below, compost heap of everything evil in our species from racial hatred to sexual guilt.

Most neurobiologists agree that the future evolution of the human species lies within the skull. If the right hemisphere of the brain stands for reason and logic as opposed to the left's perceptions, we must develop both aspects of our minds. Though we may eventually learn to communicate with each other through thought waves alone, though biofeedback may teach us to heave our headaches out of our heads and into our hands, though attendance at ashrams may help us to levitate or slow our heartbeats to release our latent anger, these are not the frontiers of mankind. The real front lines are obvious, so obvious and so challenging that they are often deliberately ignored and, by some women, even held in contempt. Thought-wave communication will do us no good if the thoughts we communicate are unreasonable, levitation is for the birds and we are already past masters at releasing our latent anger. The practice of reason can be our only hope, that most heartbreakingly difficult of skills and the purest and most lovely attribute that we have gained since we left the forests and ventured on to the plains. Reason is the new territory, the source of kindness, charity and unselfishness, the root and core of our future transformation into superhumans.

Our limits today for the unfettered indulgence of emotion are more rigid than ever before because unless we take heed of those limits we risk the destruction of ourselves and our planet. So far, women have been able to lay most of the blame on men but, with our dawning freedom to participate, it is vital that we bring with us the cold clear light of reason. There is no question of our ability to do this – and in doing so, counteract generations of male unreason – the only question lies in whether we see the dangers of irrationality or simply add to them in the name of the eternal feminine. And heaven knows, there are enough to add to. Though the powerful established religions of the West seem to have begun the slow spiral downwards into decay, many people, terrified at what they see as a yawning vacuum, rush to fill it with a mass of even more irrational beliefs. They do not wish to face a looming and inevitable truth – that we are masters of our fate, that there is no Daddy in the sky to count the hairs of our heads and that whatever our purpose in being here on earth, it is no more nor less important than the purpose (or no-purpose) of any other species on any other planet in any other universe in the infinite reaches of space.

Love may turn out to be our only solace in this loneliness of a million million galaxies but we must learn to shift its source from the tempests of the limbic system to the cool places of the neo-cortex if it is to be a true solace and not a mirage that dissolves as we get close. The loves we know (late-comers though they are) are passion and romance and both, if given the centre of the stage, will not sustain the burden of reality. Indeed, both are an escape from reality.

Romance cocoons itself in chiffon and lace, perfumes and songs and rose-coloured spectacles, to avoid any hint of the reality of the loved one that would melt the glittering bauble away. Passion puts all its energies to exaggerating reality, tightening emotional strings to the highest pitch in an all-consuming drive towards tension, drama, danger and death. Once, at its start, romance served an elegant purpose, it produced the first gentleness and reciprocity between the sexes, a brave enough attempt to supply by art what was missing in fact. Now it is past its peak and well on the way to decrepitude and romantic flourishes can be seen to have a devious purpose. Like the fine pomanders carried by seventeenth-century ladies to cover the effluvia of unwashed bodies and rotting teeth, it conveniently conceals the gangrenous patches in the relationships between the sexes, the reality of male oppression and female manipulation, the loveless and often brutal marriages and lovelessness itself. It is an insult, too, however well concealed in high-flown compliments to eyes like lakes and corn-silk hair, because if all the worshipping, the pedestals, the garters and the gages were slipped under some giant magnifying glass we would see, tucked way down there at the bottom, a tiny word-balloon that says:

> I'm looking for an angel
> To sing my love song to
> But until the day that one comes along
> I'll string along
> With you.

Thanks ever so, but no thank you. Love, used in a romantic or passionate context, is merely a licence for indulgence of our own needs and fantasies, a prop for our weaknesses and an accessory for our shaky egos. True love is, above all, an emanation of reason; a rational apprehension of another human being and a logical assessment of his or her particular needs, virtues and failings, in the light of reality. In some ways women have already understood this better than men but our subordinate position and the resulting dependency and weak sense of self have prevented us acting on it. Which is the other and perhaps the greatest obstacle of all still to be overcome in the name of love.

NINE

The Equation

'Side by side.'

Inequality is the worm in the bud of love, the viper in all our bosoms. Every single relationship between one man and one woman since women became the inferior sex has been dishonest because unequal and, to that extent, unreal. If they have lived together in the name of love all their lives, they have lived a dream because inequality is a sound barrier through which true voices are not heard. I lived with two men for seven years each and neither of them knew my true voice, which belongs to a human being and not to a member of the female sex. That is a voice still too dangerous for us to permit ourselves, at least in mixed company.

> ... that little laugh
> in the throat like a chicken bone
> that perfunctory dry laugh
> carries no mirth, no joy
> but makes a low curtsy, a kow-tow
> imploring with praying hands
> forgive me, for I do not
> take myself seriously
> do not squash me.
> That raucous female laughter
> is drummed from the belly
> it rackets about kitchens,
> flapping crows
> up from a carcass,
> hot in the mouth as horseradish
> it clears the sinuses
> and the brain ...

How many women recognize that female laughter of which Marge Piercy writes, know that voice that has another timbre entirely from the voice permitted in the world? It is the sound of freedom and, if heard too soon, could bring down the whole pack of cards. How many men recognize the same distortion in themselves, the dissimulations of an uneasy dominance?

In the long and tumultuous history of what passed for love between men and women, one thing is crystal clear. Like a precious stone badly set, it has always had its potential brilliance dulled and flawed by the claws of inequality that hold it. Whenever similarity of rank and background came closest to setting a man and a woman side by side, still the ancient rule persisted and persists: woman is for man and man is for higher things, for God.

The very matrix of love contains the deepest inequalities – powerful parent and powerless child. All of us must, as infants, experience the utmost dependency possible within a loving relationship and in that aspect the human race has never learned to put away childish things. The boy is made into the master and provider and rules, at best, with generosity. The girl merely grows, remains dependent and accepts it, at best, with gratitude. The battle of the sexes is confined within these inexorable perimeters – in the intimacy of the home the woman may strive for dominance, the man may be submissive, but in the great outdoors they are unequal again and the butt of jokes. Occasionally, a woman and a man reach a sort of mutual private treaty of equality that defies the world's view; they see beyond the stereotype and the regulations to each one's inner virtues and qualities, they hold on to these with a rare tenacity and come as close to loving truly, as equals, as the world allows.

Given the parent–child experience common to us all and the dependency of women on men, it is hardly surprising that the happiest love affairs and marriages we can achieve are, and always have been, the old reliable: father/husband and daughter/wife. Homo sapiens, during most of history, was a hierarchical creature. Domination and submission, authority and obedience, the leaders and the led, all the rituals and jockeyings for position in a vertical structure have had an important part to play in our development. Even today, when society is becoming much more flexible, many people look back with nostalgia to feudal times, when the rich man was in his castle, the poor man at his gate and everyone knew what was what and who was who. Decisions are painful, autonomy is a heavy responsibility and many of us would rather others shouldered the burden. We are still adolescents who rebel, demand freedom and independence and then, when the going gets tough, run back to our parents for shelter and protection.

In the 1890s, a young wife wrote to a friend, 'One of the great advantages of being married, you will soon find, is that you have a fount of wisdom ever springing at your side,' and the friend, Mary Vivian, later observed of her own wedding ceremony, 'I said *obey* firmly, feeling the pleasure of having no longer to order other people's lives, but to be ordered myself.' Men, on the other hand, take up the parental position. There are many examples of men who marry their wards, their god-daughters and the daughters of their friends with whom they are already *in loco parentis*; and love letters through the ages refer frequently to the male desire to 'mould' the new wife just as if he had been presented with a new-born daughter. To this end, the letters were filled with instructions to the loved one or wife, bidding her improve her mind with good books, learn how best to run an economical household and generally fit herself for the honour of being beloved. Men advised each other upon the subtleties of picking wives as they might pass on a horse-dealer's tips, get them young, the better for moulding, and obedient so that she 'be silent and learne of her husband at home'. The boring thing about wives, of course, was that they had an irritating habit of dying in childbirth, like Sir Thomas More's wife Jane, of whom Erasmus wrote, 'She was just growing into a charming life's companion for him when she died young, leaving him with several children.' The Virgin Queen's courtier Sir Walter Raleigh instructed his son, 'Have therefore ever more care that thou be beloved of thy wife rather than thyself besotted on her.' Charles Darwin, a gentle man whose marriage was long and happy, observed wryly, 'I want practice in ill-treating the female sex ... I hope to harden my conscience in time: few husbands seem to find it difficult to affect this.' Even those men who, against their own best advice, actually fell in love did not view this madness as any

162

reason to assume the woman's worth as a human being. T. H. Huxley, who fell in love with his wife at first sight, wrote to a friend, 'Love opened up to me a view of the sanctity of human nature and impressed me with a deep sense of responsibility.' None the less, he never believed in women's intellectual powers and was firmly against women's emancipation.

The most one can say of equality in love is that beauty and virtue in women have been given lip-service equality by men. If a woman was a rare beauty, then that transient characteristic went some way towards redressing the balance between the sexes and if she were particularly virtuous, then she was told that that made her not equal, but better than the world-weary male. The Marquis of Halifax, who wrote his thoughts to his daughter Elizabeth in what became the seventeenth-century best-seller *Advice to a Daughter,* acknowledged that there were inequalities between men and women and a double standard of morality but treated this as if it were ordained by God, which indeed must have seemed to be the case:

There is inequality in the sexes and that for the better economy of the world the men, who were to be the law-givers, had the larger share of reason bestowed upon them; by which means your sex is better prepared for the compliance that is necessary for the better performance of these duties which seem to be most properly assigned to it . . . You have more strength in your looks than we have in our laws and more power by your tears than we have by our arguments.

Further on, he admits that men play the sexual tyrant over women 'by making that in the utmost degree criminal in the woman which in a man passeth under a much gentler censure. The root and the excuse of this injustice is the preservation of families from any mixture which may bring a blemish to them.' He continues with advice to the woman on how best to coax the good out of her man and adds, 'The surest and most approved method of dealing with the boor is to do like a wise Minister to an easie Prince: first give him the orders you afterwards receive from him.'

This is an interesting comment because it freely admits

that the inequalities between the sexes were mirrored in life in general – all relationships were based on hierarchies of various kinds – and it underlines what these inequalities invoked: in order to survive, whether in hierarchical love or society, the ability to manipulate other human beings was mandatory. What it also makes clear is that because of inequalities, almost all relationships between men and men and men and women were functional rather than personal; in other words that they were entered into for what could be gained rather than for any more intimate pleasure.

So love has always been marred by the dependency of women upon men and men, in their turn, upon women. In the past, love or some debasement of it gained a woman her whole existence: home, family, the roof over her head, the food in her mouth and the status that she would otherwise lack. A man gained easy access to sex, a skilled and energetic servant to minister to his comforts and an incubator for his children. Today, for the majority, nothing much has changed. Even for the minority who consider themselves above such mercenary transactions, love as need is still paramount. A woman needs her lover to assuage her inner doubts, set the seal on her femininity, provide her with psychic security and give her the framework so necessary in our society – the couple, the family. A man needs his beloved for the same reasons and even for his worldly success. There are many jobs in which a man may only climb if he is respectably married; in other words he must be seen by his employer as having 'got love out of the way' and therefore in a position to devote his whole energies to earning a living. Love is a bastion against loneliness, necessary in a vast uncaring world as a method of proving one small individual identity. 'I am loved, therefore I am' would be the cry, if it were ever honestly cried.

Perhaps, then, since love has never existed without some form of dependence, dependency is an intrinsic part of love, its very woof and warp, accurate reflection of the nursery world that bred it. Is there always one who kisses and one who turns the cheek? If that functional ingredient of love, the fulfilment of needs, were to vanish as one half of lovers, the female half, becomes independent, will the whole fall apart because the centre cannot hold? Because there is nothing at the centre? Does love only grow from gratitude for things missing and supplied? Is love even possible if you want nothing from it? Will women's liberation sound the knell of love?

In the 1950s Professor Jacques Maquet published the result of his observations in Central Africa in *The Premise of Inequality in Ruanda*. There, the fact of inferiority or superiority resembled the position of men and women in the wider world, in that birth into a particular caste or tribe determined individual status for good and all. If you were born a Tutsi, you were a member of the dominant tribe, if you were born a Twa you were inferior to the Tutsi and that was for ever that. Intercaste marriage between the Tutsi and the Twa was prohibited. An attitude of submissive dependency was a permanent requirement of every Twa towards every Tutsi in every aspect of life, from personal relations to work, politics and art. Though a Twa could disagree with a Tutsi and find convincing excuses for not carrying out an order, acceptance of such behaviour could only happen if the Twa member made sure that the underlying assumption of compliance was not violated. On the other hand, the Tutsi privileges carried with them fairly heavy obligations of protection, encompassing the whole of the subordinate's life. The Tutsi were, in a sense, there to accord help to the Twa on demand and the Twa were there as the Tutsi's source of profit. From work to the furthermost recesses of personal life, the ruler was expected to aid and interfere because he was the ruler and the Twa, far from regarding this behaviour as meddling, demanded this interference as a token of his master's and care for him, and resented deeply any diminishing of this meddling, signal to him of a lack of proper paternal love. The parallel with expectations between men and women in general is obvious. Like the old Spanish proverb: the woman fears she has lost her man's love if he stops beating her. Inequalities of birth give rise to such a massive distortion of love that any treatment of the inferior by the superior is given the name 'love' and only indifference, a cessation of any interference, is seen as no-love.

Christopher Caudwell, in his *Studies in a Dying Culture*, condemns modern bourgeois society because 'tenderness can only exist between men and in capitalism all relations appear to be between a man and a commodity'. Even feudalism, even slavery was a relationship between people, however much it might at times resemble the relationship of master and dog. The slavemaster still had to come into personal contact with his slaves, the lord of the manor was necessarily involved with his peasants, so that the bad or good that came of it was at least human bad and good. Whereas today Mr Caudwell feels that cash and machines have made human contact obsolete. We work for money, not for a master, we work with machines and not with other people and a whole spectrum of human emotion, including love, withers with lack of use.

Although [slavery] was a relation, not of co-operation but of domination and submission, of exploiter and exploited, it was a human relation ... how can even that much consideration enter into the relations of a group of shareholders to the employees of a limited liability company? Or between Indian coolies and British tea drinkers? ... The threads that bind feudal lord to liege, chief to tribe, patriarch to household slave, father to son, because they are tender are strong. But those that bind shareholders to wage-employee, civil servant to tax payer and all men to the impersonal market, because they are merely cash and devoid of tender relations, cannot hold.

Clearly, then, in Mr Caudwell's view, any relationship between people is better than none and though a plantation slave might have opted for none rather than endure the cruelty of a sadistic master, any system that by definition excludes human relations throws the baby out with the bathwater – kindness with cruelty, love with hatred. Under feudalism, tribalism or slavery, men were willy-nilly thrown together and tenderness could emerge. Under capitalism, people are isolated from each other, forced to seek for all love and all tenderness from the other person in the home, and marriages begin to crack from the strain.

Obviously, Mr Caudwell feared that if dependency was removed from human relationships, particularly within a technological society, a kind of love would cease to exist and certainly there are, today, women who are no longer dependent upon men for the fulfilment of any of their needs and therefore appear to have no feeling towards them.

'What', said a friend of mine recently, 'do I want a man for? I earn more than most men, I have my own home, I have lots of friends, I don't want any children and I can repair my own fuses. If a man moved in, it would mean dirty shirts, more cooking and probably quarrels. Who needs it?'

A reaction like this is entirely new in the saga of male–female relationships. Men have been traditionally reluctant to marry on the grounds that they too could cope and why should they exchange freedom for the straitjacket of husbandry. But for them there were always incentives. A wife usually meant increased comfort – she was an unpaid housekeeper – and when the burdens of domestic life (loads of old socks lying under the bed and nothing but stuffed olives in the fridge) got too much, marriage would ensure a woman to sort it out. Besides, you could sleep with a woman whenever you wanted and she would produce the sons and heirs that were necessary to ensure the continuation of the line. Women today have no such incentives to lure them away from their self-centred freedom. Nor is there any point in using the word 'self-centred' pejoratively. For women to concentrate upon their own needs and their own wishes is still so new, so unique, that it is a kind of triumph, even though it is likely to turn sour with time. At the moment, though, it looks very much as if dependency was the glue that kept men and women together and as it disappears, so they part.

Of course, even in a society that discriminated against women, dependency was not always confined to them. Many couples stay together because the woman feels that the man is totally dependent upon her, that she is what she most craves to be, 'needed'. Alcoholism, wife-beating, a vast male irresponsibility, sometimes splits relationships but also, often, keeps them together. A woman in her sixties said to me about her bad-tempered and thoroughly unlikeable husband, with evident pride, 'Who else would put up with him?' He was her dependant, her *enfant terrible* and her reason for existence.

Dependency triggers off powerful instincts of caring without which our young would not survive. It is inappropriate for adults and – worse than inappropriate – actually stunting, but for most of our history the dependent relationship has been the only one on offer, and, being gregarious creatures, we have opted for that. It forms a sort of fail-safe device, too, always there in time of trouble for use as a cosy regression from a too harrying adulthood. If dependency were just a question of the economic facts of women's lives, prevented as they have been from earning a living or exercising adult rights and opportunities, or if it were in some way endemic to women's natures, then dependency would play no part in homosexual relationships and it quite evidently does. Most of the male homosexual couples I know divide the roles almost as carefully as if one were a woman and the other a man and yet this is quite unnecessary economically, since both have jobs. And besides this division – one does the shopping and the cooking, the other copes with bills, the car, the outside world – many take up fairly stereotyped 'female' and 'male' interests and attitudes. One goes out to the pub while the other stays home to cook the joint. One talks and the other listens. One discusses business and the other chats about books. The examples are endless and instantly distinguishable: I asked a wide sample of people about three homosexual couples known to us all – Who, if Bill and Fred were a man and a woman, would be the woman? Everyone confirmed my own views.

Economic and legal equalities, where they now exist between men and women, have not yet made much difference to inner dependencies. Kate Millet must epitomize many people's idea of a liberated woman – intelligent, creative, active, successful, independent. She fell in love with another woman who was also intelligent, active, independent and successful in her field. Equality could, it seems, go no further. But Ms Millett's anguished story of her love, described in *Sita*, shows her plumbing the depths of humiliation in her dependency upon her 'lady'; her whole life revolving around Sita, waiting for Sita to finish work, waiting to be made love to, waiting for attention, waiting for Sita's moods to pass, waiting, waiting. She even, perhaps unconsciously, puts herself in dependent situations – she leaves her own New York world to become a circling planet in Sita's San Francisco, she spends a bitter summer as a satellite in Sita's Italy, dependent even for language, for expression, upon her lover. She experiences every pang of the jailhouse of love, continually urging herself to break out, continually defeated by a smile or a minute's renewed tenderness. By any worldly standards, she is the dominant partner, by all her behaviour she shows her own conviction that she is inferior and, curiously, inferior in femininity. Sita, as Kate assesses her, has entered more wholly into the life experience of being a woman: she has had adoring husbands, she has been a proper suburban wife dependent on a man, given gifts by him, ostentatiously kept by him. She has had children. She has been raped. Even a kind of worldly dependency enters into Kate's love. Sita was born an Italian countess and awes her lover by this as only an American can be awed, particularly an American scratching around for any crumbs of superiority to pile upon her own determinedly inferior head.

Learn to say no, she taunted me last week, the phrase still like a slap. And if I did, would she cease to ask? That is what I fear, just that. So little faith in my own powers to be coy, to attract, even to distract. I who have been on hand or on tap anyway, every moment. There for her when Neal isn't, or the children, or committees or Mark or the job or the countless friends and well-wishers. I who have stood by, hangdog or carefully neutral, her shadow, her nuisance.

There are, of course, different sorts of inequalities from worldly or even inner kinds. The most independent of human beings have more or less of qualities that make them more or less equal to others. You are more intelligent than I, I am more practical than you. You are timid, I am bold. I am cheerful, you melancholy. The list is endless. In *The Rector's Daughter*, written in 1924, Flora Mayor writes:

The Herberts' was a happy marriage. It was not what the tie with Mary [Herbert's first love] would have been. They did not know what each was going to say before the words were uttered, but presumably not one husband or wife in a million do. Indeed, they were often completely astray as to what the other was driving at. The union was quite unequal intellectually. The language he spoke to her was not the language in which he thought; the life of his mind was apart from hers. He had soon given up reading English classics to her; they laughed now at the recollection.

It was owing to this intellectual disparity that Mr Herbert kept up his old friendships more than is generally the case with men who are happily married. He went now and then for a night or two to Cambridge and his relish of the talk in the Combination Room after Hall was rather too much the joy of seeing rain after drought. Mary would have been wounded. Kathy [his wife] would have thought 'Of course he wants more than I can give him, bless him,' regarding intellectual conversation as a sort of rocking horse for a beloved child.

One sees every day that unequal marriages, on whichever side the inferiority may be, are as happy as any other, happier even:

He leaned on the calm and steadfast Kathy . . . while still feeling him above her, she found he required much protecting and looking after. 'You are quaint, Crab,' she would say. 'Sometimes you seem as if you'd been in the nursery all your life.'

Once again the parental relationship wins out. In fact, a large part of the book is a description of the more typical marriage of the time, except that the participants are actually father and daughter. Spinster Mary is economically dependent upon her father, Canon Jocelyn, and from childhood emotionally dependent too. She is in awe of his learning and of him, she adores him, she cares for him, she caters to his every whim. He is usually unaware of her care and her sacrifices, spasmodically grateful, often cold. Her dependence on him and his on her (for creature comforts) merely mirror what most of her contemporaries experienced, later, in marriage.

Domination and submission, inequalities, are far older than mankind; they play an important and sometimes vital part in the survival of all animals. Certain gestures of submission, derived from the behaviour of the young animal, trigger off impulses of caring (mercy, we would call it) in the dominant animal and literally save lives, since one of two fighting males, once defeat looms, only has to ape the submissive gestures of the young to end the fight before death intervenes. Clearly, natural selection has decreed that though survival depends upon an animal's impulse to fight for territory (food, bonding) and females (fitness for breeding) such impulses, unchecked, would act against the species's best interests by slaughtering too many potentially useful peers. Fighting is genetically useful, fighting to the death is genetically wasteful, so animals who learned how to call upon submissive gestures lived and were selected because, later, they bred where the dead cannot breed. It is clear, too, that dominant and submissive behaviour is closely bound up with sexual behaviour, and often triggers it. Females 'present' themselves for mating, young animals use the same 'presenting' to older, more powerful animals to calm them and the dominant animal, apparently sexually fooled, often mounts the younger (whether male or female) in an attempt to complete the proper ritual, the cause and the effect. It seems that status, hierarchy, is as important as sex in survival, the two are inextricably bound up together and each sex uses the gestures interchangeably – dominant females 'mount' submissive females and the males do the same to each other. And in the animal kingdom, often, status is dependent upon the right sexual partner. In one experiment, a hen who was at the bottom of the pecking order in one flock was removed and mated with the dominant male of another flock. Immediately, she took his rank and became the dominant female in her new flock. Interestingly, female dominant behaviour in animals appears to be a need on its own. Males work out dominance for very obvious reasons – the dominant male or males are given the right to breed and submissiveness, at least in primates, actually deprives them altogether of that right and apparently mirrors that loss in a lowering of hormones to a level where breeding is no longer a drive, though it may become so again at any future shifting of the hierarchy. Females, on the other hand, practise dominance upon each other for no other reason than the wish for dominance itself – survival and breeding have nothing to do with it since the dominant males mate with every female in the tribe when she is on heat. That drive, it seems, is independent of the norms of selection.

Oddly enough, there are many signs in human females that submissive behaviour is not so much submissive as neutralizing, a method of evading possible enemies, or even of making friends. Men show dominant and submissive behaviour to each other in a pure 'animal' sense and in the same sense dominance lasts only as long as the submissive does not feel strong enough to challenge that dominance – the balance is delicate and constantly tested. Women, on the other hand, have traditionally used submissive gestures and behaviour as a way of evading the whole question of hierarchy, as if they had more important things to think about than this constant struggle. Much has been written about the 'promiscuous' woman, a state considered so basically unnatural as to need solutions, and perhaps it does. Or did. All sorts of guesses about the roots of her behaviour have been mooted – she is frigid and hoping for an orgasm at the end of the tunnel, she is looking for love, she is insecure about her femininity. All these may have some truth in them but my own observation seems to indicate that women's impulses towards promiscuity are directed much more towards making 'friends' or, rather, 'non-enemies' of men; as with the woman who sought relationships with all her male colleagues, the promiscuous woman sees the male as a threat and 'presents' herself to neutralize that threat.

I had a curious dream once that seemed to confirm my hypothesis. For almost a year I had been subjected to personal attack in a magazine. Week after week, month after month, in every issue the attacks continued – scandal, cartoons, innuendoes, lies. I tried to be detached and I was wretched, a vast sense of injustice and a growing paranoia haunted me. Defence of myself in letters was hopeless, I would have opened myself to even more gibes, since defence – in the ethics of that magazine – was their signal of success in driving the needle home. I had never met the editor of the magazine but I knew what he looked like from photographs.

One night, after months of this persecution, I dreamed that he fell in love with me, that we slept together. He was besotted with me, I was completely detached, I allowed him a fascinating variety of sexual favours, end of dream. My satisfaction, in the dream, was complete. I was triumphant because I knew that this one-off sexual relationship had magically taken all danger out of him, had neutralized him. Having been my lover, he was no longer an enemy. I felt nothing at all sexual, only pleasure in his defeat and my safety. Nothing could have shown me more clearly that my defence was sex, submissive sex for the purpose of eventual survival, if not actual dominance. After that, oddly enough, I was free of my previous paranoia and, even more curiously, the magazine stopped attacking me.

Status plays a very much larger part in human life than most of us are either aware of or would care to admit. It is linked with equality but there are profound differences – status is determined by the customs, the rewards and punishments of a particular society and is therefore changeable and manipulable. Forces outside the individual select the conformities upon which status will be awarded. Equality is comparatively more detached, it has no moral overtones. To say that a man is among his equals is to say nothing of his virtues or his vices, it is a statement only about his attributes vis-à-vis his fellows. Status is vertical, equality horizontal; status an acceptance of the values of a social order, equality neutral about those values. A human being who strives for status has already tacitly accepted the values of the society he hopes will confer status upon him. The person who wants merely to be equal with others seems, on the surface, less demanding, more neutral about those values but in fact challenges one of the oldest and most powerful dictates of human society and is therefore a revolutionary.

Though the drive for status presupposes a hierarchy of dominance and submission, winners and losers, in intimate relationships it requires equality up to a certain point. Marriages are traditionally made between men and women equal at least in rank, class or caste, largely on the grounds that suitable children cannot be satisfactorily bred from a female too far inferior to the male. If such an inferiority of birth does occur it is usually in cases where the female's beauty or wealth offers adequate compensation to the male. 'Always be nice to young girls,' said a Victorian dowager, 'you never know whom they may marry', and certainly part of the reason girls were kept carefully 'innocent', semi-educated and sheltered by ambitious parents was so that they could be handed over to often much older husbands as wet clay, malleable and 'upwardly mobile' because as yet unformed.

But though equal or near-equal status was desirable in the worldly ingredients of marriage, the status of the individual wife was always kept at least a notch lower than her husband's, in conformity with society's more general view of men and women. The greater age of the husband conferred an automatic status upon him, his rights vis-à-vis his wife gave him legal status as master of his household, his abilities outside the home improved his status where it might actually lower his home-bound wife's, and there was always the Church – historically willing and eager to encourage his claims to a higher spiritual status. Wives were forced to domesticate their own status drives, confining them to petty snobberies, the ostentatious spending of their husbands' money, the bearing of more sons or even, pathetically, attempting to gain spiritual status among other wives by reinforcing a husband's conviction of spiritual superiority, tending him as if he were indeed sitting on the right hand of God. Husbands and wives shared something of the same status but nothing of the same equality.

In this hierarchy, love should have been a maverick, a fly in the careful ointment, anarchy within the status quo. If we are to believe in love as surmounting all obstacles, a supreme power that overturns all social rules, an extraordinary possession descending from the gods, then the thread of love through history should show us proof. It shows us nothing of the sort. In fact, most of the evidence adds up to the clear conclusion that human beings are, consciously or unconsciously, perfectly able to control and direct love into socially acceptable channels and that that is their overriding impulse. Nothing could prove more poignantly and bleakly the way in which status overrules supposedly anarchic love than examining the mould of love itself, that earliest passion that forms, we are told, the basis for all future loves – the love of the child for the first individual who devotes her life to him or her. The mother. Or, as was the case for generations among the well-to-do (who left the records), the nurse or nanny.

To take the nanny first. Here was a woman, enshrined in the literature and lives of English infants, who was to all intents and purposes the infant's mother. Her face it was that their eyes first focused upon as it bent over their cradles, singing them to sleep or making them more comfortable, rocking them in warm arms and even feeding them from warm and ample breasts. She it was who supervised their comings and goings, wiped away their childish tears, consoled them in loneliness, crept up to see them after parental scoldings, was with them all the days of their childhood. From her arms they were released to visit, for perhaps two hours a day, their mother and father, to her arms they retreated when the visit was over, to be coaxed to bed and crooned over and told stories. Mothers sat aloof and brilliant in diamonds, too beautiful, too perfect to touch, objects of admiration from afar. Fathers were frightening, over-aweing presences, bearded replicas of Jehovah, to be worshipped in dread and in fear. Only nanny was a refuge, a human among idols, with a bosom to nuzzle and lips to kiss goodnight. Innocent of the world, many children deeply loved their nannies. But once the brain had developed enough to understand worldly things, it imposed an immediate censorship upon this deepest love and almost always succeeded in banishing it, strangling it, exorcizing it. Why? Because the nanny, the beloved, was seen as unworthy, too low in status, too unequal to be loved. Cut off by an act of will, that earliest passion atrophied, withered for lack of oxygen, and died into a pale shadow of its once supreme self – a condescending affection.

That amputation was practised endlessly, painfully but, above all, successfully, by a myriad gently-bred children on their black or white first loves. And the experience is, on the whole, uncharted, considered so 'natural', so obligatory (perhaps so shameful and agonizing) that it has been wiped off almost all records and does not even figure in the designs of that cartographer of the human soul, Sigmund Freud. Nor was this amputation in the interests of status always confined to servants. Mothers, too, were often rejected because they were also considered 'unworthy', lower of status than the father and therefore not to be loved too much, particularly by daughters whose own potential status was threatened by their common femininity.

If the very foundation of love is thus manipulable, it is perhaps not so surprising, though irremediably tragic, that the black races enslaved by the British and Americans could have been made to adopt the status symbols of their masters in love, and in doing so reject for perhaps three hundred years the love between black women and black men. The befrilled, perfumed and leisured white woman was presented by the white master to his black slaves as the only fit object for love and lust and, taking her as the ideal, the black man found his own slave sisters wanting. Add to that the deliberate British colonial policy of breaking up family and tribal ties amongst slaves for fear of allowing any sort of rebellious cohesion, plus the colonialist's need to have more black slaves and the product is a final degradation – black man sees himself as stud and the black woman as breeder.

The black woman, regarded as a work-horse, a producer of new slaves and a transient sexual repository by her white owner, could not be defended by either black lover or father from random rape and ill-treatment and both were forced into seeing her through the white man's eyes by their own impotence, their continually degraded virility. As the men were driven into irresponsibility the women grew contemptuous of them; wives and mothers would do anything to protect their menfolk but the price of such protection was an inevitable distancing. Each sex, in the battle for survival, had to sacrifice the mutual equality of slavery for the artificial barriers of status – house slaves were set against field slaves, women thought men idle good-for-nothings, men called their women tramps and whores. To this day, the

manipulation of slave love shows its horrid marks of success –
by his own admission Eldridge Cleaver 'practised' rape upon
black women before he turned to his ultimate aim, the rape
of white women; and West Indian men, in England and at
home, often have several families of erstwhile mistresses and
children who support themselves.

There were, throughout this black history, examples of
individuals who courageously refused to conform in love and
broke all social taboos in reaching across the colour bar.
Society turned a half-blind eye to illicit sexual relationships
between white masters and their black female slaves but a
few Southern gentlemen cared enough for their concubines
to try to will them money and property after death, a process
that is confirmed in Catterall's *Judicial Cases* which sets
forth the efforts of white relatives to deny slave mistresses
and their children such inheritances. A few white men even
attempted what was virtually impossible at the time, to
marry a black woman. In a classic Revolutionary love affair,
a British soldier, nursed back to health by a free mulatto
woman and her daughter, fell in love with the daughter and
found he could not legally wed her. When a doctor came to
bleed her for some minor ailment, he drank a few drops of
her blood and marched off to the town hall to sign an
affidavit saying that he had coloured blood in him. Thus he
was given a marriage licence. But the vast majority conformed to the edict and found no trouble in controlling love
across colour barriers, however much they might satisfy
their lust in that direction.

Nor is this dislike of loving 'below one's station' confined
to such high barriers as race. The results of one survey into
the choosing of marriage partners established that most
people marry others who live in an astonishing five-block
range of the parental home and that the partners are overwhelmingly likely to be very similar in background and
financial resources. Another survey carried out by the University of Florida showed that a whopping 85 per cent of
dating couples picked at random in bars and theatre lobbies
were paired to within one point of a five-point scale rating of
physical attractiveness, which seems to prove a drive

towards equality even in looks, which are never rated very high when people are asked what attributes they would like to see in hypothetical partners. Many of the recent surveys emphasize how much love is bound up with similarities of views and attitudes on a range of subjects from politics to astrology – a point accepted by almost all marriage bureaux and computer dating companies who aim to match like and not unlike pairs. All this can, of course, be explained away for other reasons – for instance, a man may well be attracted by a woman far better looking than himself and decide not to approach her for fear of rejection, but if he can redress the balance by increasing his own contributions of wealth, social position or talent, one such imbalance may make no difference. Evidently, though we like to think that falling in love is entirely irrational, part of our minds acts like a dedicated book-keeper, busy adding and subtracting a list of debits and credits each time we meet a member of the opposite sex and ticking or crossing off those who, combined with us, would not balance the books.

Ian Suttie, 1930s author and psychologist, had a fascinating theory of the way in which the inequality of women lay at the root of the much-quoted Oedipus complex, Freud's blueprint of a son's struggle to suppress sexual desire for his mother out of fear of his father's revenge and his replacement of that desire by identifying with the father's power and authority. Suttie reasoned that the original desire of the son for his mother arose partly, at least, from the fact that in a patriarchal society he saw her as inferior to his father and therefore a kind of equal to himself. Most mothers will recognize some truth in this. Because many husbands count themselves lords of their household, the wife and children are lumped together as his underlings, catering for his needs. When the husband is particularly authoritarian (in Freud's nineteenth-century Vienna, for instance) wife and children amuse themselves together as equals and warn each other to behave when the man returns – mice playing while the cat is away. The mother complicates the situation by treating her son as she has learned to treat powerful adult males, deferring to him, showing him her helplessness, even behaving with a mild flirtatiousness. Thus the son is encouraged in his desire for her, fears his father as an avenging God and so the Oedipal struggle is set in motion.

Suttie reasoned that if the mother's inequality did not exist, Oedipus would never rear his divisive head. Given equal status with men by society, she would be seen by her son as unequal with him. Given a role to play in a wider world than the nursery, she herself would see her son as a child rather than an ambiguous equal. Effectively beyond her son's reach, her own needs satisfied among her peers, she herself can authoritatively nip his infant lust in the bud and at the same time take the sting out of the father–son relationship. This is probably exactly what happened in ancient matriarchies, at least according to the testimony of legend and ritual, and as women become equal with men in our world we can begin, however vaguely, to discern something of the same changes. In the West it is already true that in many families children no longer feel the old half-fear, half-worship that the authoritarian father provoked and there is a growing tolerance, sexual freedom and lack of guilt that signifies, perhaps, lack of the suppressed Oedipal wish to kill the father. Many young people these days seem to feel equality in their bones in a way that is unique in history and that, too, could be the result of slow changes in the family structure as well as wider changes. The essence of the Oedipal struggle is the desire to take over the powerful father's role and the essential prerequisite is an acceptance of that role as right and proper. To accept a status quo and merely to seek one's increased status in it is a very different proposition from the impulse towards democracy.

But all of these facts, surmises and plain guesses rest on a central supposition – that equality between men and women (men and men, women and women) is an essential if they are to love each other freely rather than with strings attached. There have been so few instances of this kind of loving in the past that this, in itself, is some proof that inequality, women's dependence upon men, was the final barrier against love. Equality in love is not simply an abstract principle, nice work if you can get it. It is indivisible from true love and without it we are still living in the Dark Ages, coping as best we can with a pale shadow of what love could be.

Oliver Goldsmith wrote in the eighteenth century, 'Friendship is a disinterested commerce between equals; love, an abject intercourse between tyrants and slaves', but love too, if it is ever to reach its full potential, must be as disinterested as friendship and Goldsmith's key word here is 'equals'. It is a sad thing that friendship and 'Platonic' love, both considered less important in our present obsession with the couple and sex, actually contain more of the future necessities of love than what is known as love today. Perhaps, unconsciously, we already know this – hence the oft-repeated truism that if you introduce sex into friendship you will ruin that friendship. The distrust of sex is well founded because the sexual tie, in an unequal relationship, is the key to a Pandora's box of needs, dishonesties and manipulatory neuroses.

Human beings need other human beings to survive and the kinder word for 'usefulness' is 'co-operation'. To co-operate with others for our own individual good means we must subordinate or simply neglect parts of our personality in order to achieve an end that will benefit all of us. We cannot be fully 'ourselves', though we may feel among equals, at board meetings or shareholders' meetings, trades union discussions, planning committees or any kind of co-operative effort from building a new swimming bath to the local parent–teachers' association. In such endeavours we present those parts of ourselves that are useful to others in order to get something done that will eventually be useful to us. But in order to express our full selves, to be what we are and to discover who we are, we must be among disinterested equals.

Every inequality downgrades the relationship, however slightly, into something functional. Only if you are with someone for no other reason than that you wish to be with them, can equality between you be said to exist. Indeed, equality is the only assurance that you are free to express the whole of yourself, that you need suppress nothing for reasons of expediency and you need pretend to nothing for fear of losing status. The very essence of the relationship is this full expression, that is what it is for.

A vital factor in an equal relationship is that each person within it must be able to function independently, without need of any basic kind for the other. When people talk of men and women being 'complementary' or being 'two halves of a whole', they are using pretty euphemisms for dependency. As long as men cannot manage children, cook food, iron clothes and generally cope with servicing themselves, or assume that others should do such things for them, they will be dependent upon women and as long as women cannot do the practical repair jobs or maintain themselves economically, they are dependent upon men. The division of inner resources by gender – emotion to women, rationality to men – also leads to dependency; since both sexes need to express them, both will, if forbidden to do so, manipulate the other to achieve a vicarious expression. No woman is more dependent than the one society labels a 'true woman' and no man more than the macho, he-man type. Totally unbalanced, they can only survive by suppressing large parts of themselves and refusing to allow any partner to develop for fear of too great a challenge.

Of course, the 'glue' of dependency is very strong and if the aim of society is simply to keep a man and a woman together as long as they both shall live, then dependency works as well as, and maybe a whole lot better than, disinterested love. Couples, whether married or unmarried, are a social institution and as long as we are brought up to feel that success in love is measured by long-term physical sharing of the same residence, even marriage lines can be dispensed with in a more permissive society without much change in the basic emotional structure. As long as I can be made to feel uneasy about how I direct my emotions, where I love, then I am not free and if I am not free, then I am involved in a functional and not a disinterested relationship. We can all cite couples who are, in the world's eyes, most satisfactorily glued together by dependency. The large majority still have the glue of the woman's lack of training in supporting herself and her growing fear, over the years, that she has lost even the small ability she once had. Some couples are almost equal in their dependencies. I know an elderly couple who have been married for ever. She wanders about during the day, dusting a bit, cooking a bit, her shoulders stooped, her step without spring. Come five o'clock and she sits herself down in an armchair with her eye on the front door. At the sound of the key turning in the lock, her eyes brighten, her back straightens. In comes her husband and, within minutes, the air is full of recriminations. Ding dong, you dirty swine, you filthy bitch, bang bang, shout, shriek, this is it, this time you've gone too far, this time I'm leaving. Her cheeks are pink, her eyes sparkle, even the decorous white curls on her head bounce and nod happily. The husband, too, appears to be fighting fit. Each has, over the years, made each other an adrenalin addict, each is a pusher for the other. Their friends are by turn shocked, resigned and then amused – what can you do with them, they love it, they'll be together till they drop dead. But though the stranglehold they have on each other may endure until hell cools, it is not love.

Another woman, only recently married, is immensely flattered and continually boasts about her husband's jealousy. 'John's so *jealous*,' she says, blushing prettily. 'Why, last week we went to a party given by a man I've known for donkey's years and he kissed my cheek as we came in. Well, John's sulked for almost a week since.' She offers this information as if it were the highest of compliments and indeed John's jealousy (and her own reaction) is already hardening into the bond that may keep them together for years. But whatever the source of John's jealousy, insecurity, status, even a pathological state, it is not love. In their book *Sex and Status*, Doris and David Jones cite another couple's relationship:

Aimee had been able to cope with life fairly adequately until she met Allen. She had managed to support herself and her two children and had even helped one of them through college. But with Allen on the scene the necessity for her to cope with her problems was removed. Step by step she has relinquished all responsibility, first for her own support, then for adult duties and now finally for her own health and well-being. Aimee satisfied Allen's emotional needs with her dependence . . . he hurries home from work to cook for her, he does the shopping for her on the way, he washes up and tidies for her and he telephones her every couple of hours during his working day to make sure she is all right. His sense of her absolute dependency upon him seems to have intensified the pleasure he derives from their intimacies.

Oddly, the authors sum up these dependent relationships thus:

Plainly, outsiders who criticize these relationships have an ideal in their minds. Perhaps the ideal derives from childhood stories that end with the words 'and they lived happily ever after' or from the even earlier feelings of peace of the suckling infant. But we discover that life does not always reflect our ideals. We find bonds between those whose sexual and status needs tie them together in apparent disharmony as indissoluble as between those who are bound by tenderness . . . we cannot even say whether it is desirable or not desirable, good or bad. All we can say is that this is how life is.

But it is only how life is if you assume that how life is means staying together, that the 'glue' is all-important and not *what* the glue glues. You don't have to be an idealist to realize that these relationships, indissoluble as they may be, are not about love but about needs. So brainwashed are most of us by the idea that two individuals living together are better than one, no matter how those two actually relate, that we blind ourselves to the functions served and call it, all-embracingly, 'love'. If people choose to stay together for whatever reasons, that is their business, though the word 'choose' is not altogether apt, since many have no choice. But to call their relationship 'love' is simply inaccurate and, worse, creates an image of love that debases the emotion itself. So debases it that children who grow up within a parental relationship of one or another variation of dependency can have no image of what love could actually be and therefore no aspirations towards it. Almost mechanically, they reproduce in their own coupling the same loveless ties as their parents and if they, too, manage to stagger through the years, deforming and maiming each other, they may well receive the world's accolade at the end of that time. They were 'in love'. George Orwell invented a language called Newspeak, which operated on the idea that if you eliminated certain words from normal currency, the emotion the words labelled would disappear as well. His point was that unexpressed emotion atrophies. But Newspeak can also destroy by using words indiscriminately – labelling jealousy, aggression, fear, insecurity and other emotions 'love' so that love itself falls into disrepute. As it has.

If you are to reveal yourself, warts and all, to another human being – and this is an essential part of growth, as well as being necessary for mental health – self-preservation demands that that person has no reason to use your vulnerabilities against you. Any inequality provides an ulterior motive to do just that. An 'inferior', whether by class, caste, employment or simply in the world's eyes at the time, might be a true friend and confidant unto death but there are very many reasons why he or she should not be; and if, for instance, a livelihood is dependent upon a 'superior', the motives for using that friendship are heightened.

Between 'superior' men and 'inferior' women, the same distrust occurs, foundation for the battle between the sexes. Many a woman does not receive the full confidence of a husband because he knows, however much that knowledge may be concealed, that the relationship is a dependent one and that if a crunch comes, her economic survival may oblige her to use her knowledge against him. For the same reason, women conceal things from their husbands – there is too much at stake for them to afford such intimacies. The friends of both partners in a marriage or 'love' relationship often know far more about the true feelings and actions of a husband or wife than each knows about the other and divorce hearings daily reveal the dangers of once-private confidences. In any unequal relationship, the two concerned must devote a precious amount of energy simply to jockeying for position and the relationship devolves from a frank exchange to a tiring and constricting conflict of strategies. It is not easy to be honest with an equal who has no reason to use your weaknesses. How much more difficult if the motive is clearly there.

The first and most obvious barrier to the love of sexual partners is economic inequality. Though we may dislike admitting it, there is no one thing in all our lives that so influences, changes or distorts our characters and actions as money – too little or too much or more than someone else. Woolworth heiress Barbara Hutton's autobiography is a horrifying saga of the way in which her vast fortune, which made almost every human being who came into contact with her a monetary unequal, deformed every ordinary spring of human affection into manipulative greed. Because of money, she could not believe in any gesture of disinterested kindness of love towards her; when she encountered it she was driven to test it with money and in doing so, inevitably twisted it. Because of money, ordinary people became greedy and, almost against their wills, were seduced into exploiting her. A young bell-boy in one of the many hotels where she holed up ran errands for her, without knowing who she was, in a normal spirit of helpfulness, expecting a little payment, perhaps, but prepared to put himself out a good deal. She paid him but she paid him far too much; in doing so she fed a dormant greed; he began trying to exploit her and she was confirmed in her cynicism. When a doctor attended her for a minor ailment he felt driven, because she was Barbara Hutton, into taking dramatic measures where a mere prescription of rest would have sufficed. So did many other doctors. In the end, she underwent some twenty entirely useless and unnecessary operations either out of medical greed or because of natural enough fear on the doctor's part that they were not doing enough for her. She could not believe that any man or any of her husbands loved her for herself because she could not see herself apart from the money she was sure attracted them. In much the same way, Howard Hughes, the world's richest man, suffered years of mental misery and died of physical diseases that need not have proved fatal had his wealth not isolated him. Some of the most desirable and essentially lovable men and women in the world have choked love to death with the suffocating weight of their wealth.

These examples come from the rarefied world of the very, very rich. Sadly, love has almost as little chance of survival under far smaller inequalities, as long as one of the lovers has or earns either more money than the partner or is the only monied partner of two. Take a typical couple in 1978, a couple I know living in London. Both are intelligent, educated people, equals to all intents and purposes except, by an accident, earning power. He is a geologist employed by a big oil company, she is an art historian. Big oil companies pay a lot more than museums so he earns perhaps three times more than his wife. What difference can this make? Both work a full-time week, both salaries are well-earned in dedication and effort – can the outside economics of the market place which gives oil companies the ability to pay large salaries and denies the same facility to museums possibly make a difference between them? Yes, indeed it can. The wife is aware that a large part of their shared standard of living depends on the husband's salary, that left alone she would be unable to afford what she now takes for granted. He, too, is aware of this – his wife, he realizes, could manage the necessities of life without him but none of the frills. So what happens? Without a word said between them about the crux of the matter, he slowly becomes the more cosseted member of the family, deferred to by wife and children, let off domestic chores, allowed to make most of the decisions. His wife continues to do most of the buying, including the frills, but when she buys the frills she lies about their price – I was with her when she bought a £35 palm, which was reduced, in his presence, to £5. As more authority was given him in the family, he became more authoritarian. Now the whole atmosphere of the house changes when he comes home, he is even, at times, extremely rude to his wife, perhaps in oblique protest at the authority he has been awarded. Time, energy, dedication, even the worth of jobs no longer enters their thoughts – he earns more and the winner takes all.

The majority of young mothers, stay-at-homes looking after their children, are totally dependent on their husbands' salary and have not the smallest right to any part of it, in spite of their full-time housework. Unequal and financially dependent, they slowly become dependent in everything, some of them revert to childhood in their dealings with the husband, cajoling prettily for the necessities of life, suppressing almost all their true emotions from anger to sex. In twenty years I have never met a couple where the husband is the sole wage-earner and the wife reveals her real self to him. She lives on subterfuges, concealments and falsities, small or very large. He senses these and takes refuge in rage, suspicion or a bland refusal to show interest. Quite often, his sense of superiority makes him deride her opinions, snap at her behaviour or, at best, treat her as a spoilt daughter. If the shoe is on the other foot, as it sometimes is today, and the woman is either the major or the sole earner, another kind of suppression takes place. Many working-class women whose husbands have felt the full brunt of increasing unemployment go to great lengths to conceal from everyone, even themselves, that it is the woman's money that is running the household. Because a woman earns and her man does not, that inequality is considered by both an aberration, out of the natural order of things. He becomes more domineering, she more cringing or vice versa, inequalities made manifest.

Younger and very successful women may suffer from the same lop-sided problems. A woman I know, twenty-eight years old, pretty and talented, has a demanding job and a desirable live-in unemployed boyfriend. But instead of asking him to do the shopping and the cooking for his keep, she takes on two jobs and copes at home as well as at work. In this situation, the woman has the money and the man is dependent upon her and so unequal. But his attraction as a heterosexual male who is 'kind' to successful women (i.e. does not punish his mistress for daring to make him financially unequal) is so great it redresses the balance and tips it his way. He is superior because he is in demand. She must resent this secretly but because of her inequality, her fear that he will leave her for another woman if she reveals her resentment, she keeps quiet and love takes another beating.

Disparity of intelligence or background are other types of inequality that often make love impossible. George Gissing, the Victorian novelist, had a lifelong belief that struggling professional men should not marry the well-educated middle-class girls who were their class and intellectual equals, though still dependent because unable to earn their own living. These girls, he felt, would be bound to be miserable upon the little money their husbands could provide and the husband would find himself crippled in his career by the constant need for money to keep his wife in the proper conditions. He advocated – for sexual relief and some companionship – the humble working-class girl as wife. Twice he followed his own advice, with disastrous results, and in his book *New Grub Street* he wrote of his own predicament in the persons of Alfred Yule, a struggling writer, and his working-class wife, whom he begins to treat as a servant and who lets herself be so treated because she feels inferior.

His marriage proved far from unsuccessful; he might have found himself united to a vulgar shrew; whereas the girl had the great virtues of humility and kindliness. She endeavoured to learn of him, but her dullness and his impatience made this attempt a failure; her human qualities had to suffice. And they did, until Yule began to lift his head above the literary mob. Previously, he often lost his temper with her, but never expressed or felt repentance of his marriage; now he began to see only the disadvantages of his position and, forgetting the facts of the case, to imagine that he might well have waited for a wife who could share his intellectual existence. Mrs Yule had to pass through a few years of much bitterness . . .

Bitterness that included the attempt by her husband 'scarcely to permit his wife' to talk to their child, so strong was his dread that the child would be infected with her mother's faults of speech and behaviour. Yet Mrs Yule feels her own inferiority so deeply that she treats her daughter as a superior and is constantly amazed that so low a creature as herself has managed to produce a proper lady. Understandably, Mrs Yule remains an enigma, revealing nothing of herself at all except a bewildered expression and a few dropped aitches.

The whole and real horror of inequality in love is that it always renders the relationship functional, by inhibiting or distorting the real expression of personality and increasing manipulation. The superior forces the inferior into deviousness and concealment, the inferior forces the superior into becoming a dictator, expressing only those parts of the personality associated with power. Because there is no balance, neither can exert a proper pressure on the other to achieve maturity, they stunt each other's growth instead of extending it and the result is either permanent distortion or a break-up of the relationship as one or the other explodes out of the straitjacket.

One of the vital necessities for all human beings is the attempt to 'know thyself', to discover our own individual identities, and this can only be done among other people – like bats, we bounce the echo of ourselves off others in order to know where we are. Inequality is a vacuum, it creates unreal people who deform other people's echo soundings. Only two people who love each other in total independence can create the conditions that allow self-discovery, because only they can provide properly built walls for each other's sounding. To take a very mundane example: a man asks his wife if she would like the window open or shut. She is used to deferring to him, so she says, 'Whatever you like, dear.' So he opens the window and she freezes. He is deprived by her subservience of an informed decision as to whether his or her needs are greater in this particular instance, and she catches pneumonia. In any such ordinary decision of life, from windows to political principles, when one partner conceals wishes out of dependency and fear the other develops an unreal picture of the normal elements necessary to decision and so decisions are made without either facing up to the missing elements. Automatically he begins to make them all as they suit him and she begins to harbour resentments that can turn to hate. So much can inequality colour love that for generations dependent women have been unable even to tell their husbands or lovers what gives them pleasure in sex, for fear of losing them. They prefer to pretend orgasms and so their mutual sex life drifts into illusion – the man believing that they are both perfectly satisfied. Dealing in unrealities of this order makes a mockery of memory and events and turns relationships into one of those yellow magazine headlines, 'She Lived a Lie'.

The inequalities of love, particularly within marriage, have often succeeded in driving the partner with some freedom of action – usually the man – into the arms either of men friends in whom he can confide with some honesty or other women. Most people yearn for some truth in a relationship and however dominating they may be they also want some equals around them because they feel intuitively the necessity of 'knowing' rather than guessing what others think of them and how their actions are really judged. Tycoons may surround themselves with sycophants but they call their eager inferiors 'yes-men' with contempt and even frustration. And so powerful is the human need for self-expression that a man may set up a bevy of mistresses so that in each one he can confide a particular truth about himself but tells no one of them the whole truth, on much the same principle of safety as organizations who keep each 'cell' of conspirators ignorant of all but a fraction of information so that the whole truth is known only to a mysterious Mr Big. And Mr Big, because he has no equals and, therefore, no checks on his behaviour nor access to reality, easily drifts off into a monstrous fantasy that presages his downfall. Women's subservience has taken a dreadful toll from men in much the same way.

It comes to this. Equality is not a highly recommended method of attaining stability or stasis, either politically or in personal relationships. Whether the aim is an immutable and predictable society, or a lifelong union of couples, inequality and its resulting dependencies will do a much better job of producing it than equality. For nearly one thousand years, between the fall of Rome and the end of the Middle Ages, hierarchy reigned supreme and the dependency of one human being on another reached its apogee. But it seems that in all that time, though practical inventions flourished, nothing happened that much concerned the way humanity thought or felt. Huge inequalities between man and man produced a socially half-dead world. The drive for equality, on the other hand, often presages chaos, disruption and unhappiness for society and for the individuals caught up in it but it is the only thing that offers creativity, growth and change – the imperatives of evolution. And the macrocosm of the outer world mirrors the microcosm of individual relationships – you cannot fight for equality in the world and go home to defer to a husband or fight for equality in marriage and see nothing wrong with slavery. It is, after all, no accident that the American battle for civil rights triggered the battle for women's liberation. Equality is contagious, by its nature it cannot be contained.

Curiously, too, equality is the only bedrock upon which real human worth can be built, upon which a truly admirable inequality can thrive. The so-called superiority of any human being or race or class or creed is totally unreal, a fantasy, if it is based upon an enforced inferiority of other human beings, races, classes or creeds. The claim to male superiority cannot possibly be judged until women have equal opportunities with men, just as white (or upper class or, for that matter, Christian) superiority remains untested until no taint of second-class citizenry remains. In other words, in intimate human ties as in broader relationships, we cannot know the truth until we have shed all obvious inequalities.

Love is no exception to this rule, it is the political shrunk to domestic size. How can I say I love you if I don't know who you are? And I won't know who you are until equality allows you to expose your true self, without fear of some functional loss. How can I be loved for myself alone if I belong to a ruling sect, with the power to dispense favours and influence other people's lives? What is 'my true self, myself alone'? I cannot know even that unless I can judge myself by all other human beings, who are my peers. Equality does not guarantee happiness in love, any more than inequality, but it is a gamble towards that happiness and not away from it. At least if you do achieve love in equality your achievement is built on a rock and not on quicksand.

TEN

The Future

'I never promised you a rose garden.'

By the time I met my third husband, I had experienced most of the emotions that today pass for love. As the song goes:

> At seventeen
> I fell in love quite madly
> With eyes of a tender blue
> At twenty-four
> I got it rather badly
> For eyes of a different hue
> At thirty-five
> I flirted rather sadly
> With two or three or more
> But when I thought that I was past love
> It was then I met my last love
> And I loved him as I'd never loved before.

It wasn't that my last love obliterated all the others in one huge heart-stopping tidal wave or was so magnified a version that it shrank each previous love into a pale shadow of itself. It did not vary only in degree. This love showed me quite clearly that the emotions and ties that had existed before, though often very strong, were not love at all.

My first two marriages reflected with a disturbing neatness the way things had been and the appropriate emotions. I had learned inequality at my mother's knee and my first husband replaced father in a replica of the family. Then child-wife began to grow up and lurched into another unequal parental scene, little mother to big son. There was no room for growth because the space available was just enough to fit a role and not an individual. I could have remained in one or other of these prisons for ever, to be congratulated upon love's triumph on a golden anniversary and perhaps, by then, I would have been too anaesthetized to do anything but nod and smile. But I was luckier than some. I began to work in the outside world.

Incarcerated in a house with one man, a woman can lose herself in a fantasy world. In her husband's biased eyes she is the most beautiful creature on earth, or the ugliest; the worst slut or a veritable Mrs Beeton; a mad and nagging witch or the sunniest soul since Polyanna. One man provides her with the stuff of her life, colours or discolours all about her so that she ends with no idea of her own truths. Many women have said to me, as I have said to them, when marriage ended – I am not as bad as he thought, not as bad-tempered, not as neurotic, not as plain.

In marriage I have been called a whore, a bitch, mean, selfish, frigid, mad. I have also been told that I cooked like a dream, that I was the sexiest thing ever, that I was a miracle of goodness, that I was the best mother since Marmee, that my leaving would mean their death, that I was God's gift. I shrieked and wept at the insults and smirked and blushed at the compliments but only now can I say with utter conviction and some regret that I am none of these things. These are the weapons used to hurt, to soothe and to flatter and they are only effective if you have no access to the truth. Later I learned that the kind of love I knew was inevitably distorted, had an integral flaw that twisted the image into something too grand or too grotesque to believe, like the funny mirrors in a fair. The flaw was there because the eye shifted outside reality to fit.

But when you work, strangers regard you with clear eyes, unclouded with neurotic needy love. If you can make your way there, in that cool air, you cannot help but gain a knowledge of where you are and who you are, a sense of proportion, an identity that can only be forged through others. It is sad, in a way, to have to measure yourself against comparative strangers, to assess drawbacks and advantages in the cold light of unlove but because, today and yesterday, love between men and women has been so much merchandise, prop, stimulant or placebo, we cannot find ourselves in each other unless we do not love.

Or unless we are equal and love. My third husband has

none of the attributes of a mythic lover. He is not chivalrous, he is not even very polite. He cannot dance, he is tone-deaf and colour blind, he has no moods, he does not day-dream, he does not dream at all. He brings home no flowers, he remembers no birthdays, he does not try a little tenderness. He has no god, he worships no one, loyalty is not a word he recognizes. He does not know the meaning of romance, or care to know. He never says don't worry your pretty head about it. He loves me for what is lovable in me and distances himself from what is not. He looks at me carefully with the world's eyes as well as the eyes of love, I know him to be right in his assessment and so I know where I am. He shows me to myself. If I ask him a question he will answer it as truthfully as he can and if the truth hurts he will comfort me, for a while.

He reminds me of an old wart-hog I once saw in an African twilight. Heavy-chested, heavy-breathing, it came out among the lithe deer and the noble lions gathered at a drinking hole like a Caliban among Ariels. Head down, it shunted and butted its way through the reeds, ignoring the other animals, unaware of the moonlit landscape about it, wanting only one thing. Water. My husband does the same in the landscape of love. He shunts and butts through the verbiage, unaware of the pretty scenery, ignoring the startled, sometimes angry, sometimes timorous people around him, intent on only one thing. The truth, such as it is.

He noses it out eventually but he gives it no moral coding when he has it. He does not say that's good or that's bad or try to tailor it to fit some preconception. He just wants to know what it is, as near as can be ascertained, because the truth is a grail without holiness, the only firm piece of ground in a swamp, where something could be built. He is not interested in the nice surfaces of things and so my nice surfaces dissolve when he is there. And because he loves me and not the surface me, he helps me to love myself so that I become better at loving him and others.

My husband and I both earn the same money at, as it happens, the same jobs. Both of us run our own working lives, take our own responsibilities for these and cope with our own failures. We share our money and the domestic chores, we do not necessarily share our friends or all our spare time or all our opinions. There is no area in which I secretly feel superior to him (except I make better scrambled eggs) and he says the same of me (but he makes better baked beans). This equality is not a recipe for unending bliss, as you will know if you live in the same way. It produces its own tensions and confusions and it can be very exhausting, particularly when, in moments of weakness, early conditioning pops up and whispers seductive things to the woman about the blessings of dependency (I could be a kept woman with nothing to do all day but paint my nails and look pretty) and to the man about slippers in front of the fire (where the hell are my shirts?). Nor can a couple attempting equality expect much yet in the way of encouragement from the outside world. Legislation, from that point of view, often seems to reward female dependence with easy money and all the other comforts of conformity and though the man gains a certain buoyancy through not having to support a woman financially or mentally, he may become a target for snide sexual innuendoes and he has none of the undeniable pleasure of laying down the law. We have found that other people are often deeply reluctant to see us as separate. If I annoy someone, he or she will sometimes try to embarrass my husband with my behaviour, make him obliquely apologize for me, make him admit that we are, after all, one flesh. If he is required for some project, I am often approached, on the grounds that I will influence him. The underlying assumption is always that we somehow control each other, live each other's lives, that we are not two people but a trunk with two heads, sharing all our vital organs, two hearts beating as one.

But it is our separateness, and two people's separateness within love, that is our gift to each other and you cannot be separate if you are unequal. One or other must lean more heavily, be more helpless and therefore of less help. Contrary to the old wives' tales, the real joy of love lies in the knowledge that your lover could manage without you, that he or she has no *need* of you but simply feels a great deal happier that you are there. Knowing that is also to know that when you have some problem that upsets or saddens you, this person who is also your lover can aid and advise you because there is no ulterior motive to muddy the judgment, no hunger to manipulate, no hidden fears or jealousies to twist into deviousness. Out of a true concern and a true understanding of you, a lover can help as no one else can because to love a person means to want that person to become more of that person. Until now, love has too often meant a slow chipping away or plastering up of an original model formed in the lover's eyes: I want you to feel unsure because then you will need me, I want you to flirt with others because then they will recognize what I don't quite recognize – how lucky I am to have you. Such games are endless but they are not love games.

Inner growth, that uniquely human impulse and burden, is forced to take place and given room to do so in true love. Lies of any kind, however white, are anathema, not because of the lover's high-falutin code of behaviour but simply because a lie prevents you knowing the truth, who it is you love. Being truthful is a profoundly practical thing. It permits others to love you for yourself and it allows you to know who you are. I lied to my husband when I met him, telling him I was four years younger than I was. Rooting, grunting, shoving, he kept his head down until I confessed and the relief was just the first of many such, a gust of pure happiness that he knew and still loved. With unequals you must always lie a little, if only to save them pain. Equals know that pain is part of growing, believe each other strong enough to stand what is necessary and, by believing, give that strength. This applies as much to the minefield of outside sexual encounters as anything else. True love (and self-knowledge) accepts that one person cannot provide everything for another – indeed, there is a kind of obscenity in the very notion. We live in a world crowded with others, some of whom can give you or your lover their own particular gifts and to think otherwise is to fall back, once again, into the illusion of being Mummy or Daddy with an infant, all powerful, all-nourishing. Novelty, they say, is the greatest aphrodisiac and for many people that is true and love cannot necessarily continue to provide novelty through the years. Today, many couples break up, with all the resulting misery for both of them and their children, just because one or the other partner refuses to encompass sex outside or because an extra-marital affair has been discovered in spite of careful lies. It is not easy to continue, at least with any serenity, but it is easier from a position of equality than from dependency and easier still if the love between the partners is real, based on true knowledge of the other's worth and a profound awareness of their individual existence, quite apart from you. Besides, to be extremely practical, what have you gained if you force anything, even faithfulness, on another person? Their presence, perhaps, but who wants a body with a mind elsewhere? What is the point of trying to coerce what cannot be coerced? Love does not 'allow', 'permit' or 'forbid' or it is not love. Nor, of course, does love imply some awful wish to sacrifice oneself. Once that is done, there is no one left to love. Obviously, true love founded on equality does not automatically turn two people into saints. Hurt can still be given, felt and shown – if necessary in good old-fashioned rows and flying dishes. No one is forced to suppress hurt for fear of having the very bread taken out of the mouth. But at least there is less need to lie and lies ruin everything, leaving nothing but rubble behind because what you thought happened didn't happen, what you thought didn't happen, did, and the person you thought you loved wasn't that person at all. And in that case, who the hell are you?

Growth is a facing of oneself full frontally naked and the best way to face it is in a true lover's eyes. The false lover will send you back his own carefully constructed image and you will find yourself no further on the journey. A true lover will reflect exactly who you are, with warmth at the edges to take away the sting and cheer you on the way. That truth is not always palatable and we may try to defend ourselves from it by attacking the weaknesses of the other. Unequals always have a protective bolt-hole, equals never do because, in the end, they realize that the other has no motive but their good.

Oddest of all, true love has its surest foundation in what is often thought of as the antithesis of love. In order to give and get the best of it, no individual must make it the centre of life. Love is *not* the only thing that matters at all – at its very finest it is a by-product, a side-effect, a spin-off. Like the gold at the end of the rainbow, it cannot be found by looking for it but can be tripped over on the journey to somewhere else, and wonderfully illuminate that journey. As the eighteenth-century German poet Novalis said, 'Once a woman is man's equal, she cannot be his goal.' And love cannot be found, either, before the self is found. Christianity tells us we must love selflessly and in doing so has destroyed generations of potential lovers. The truth is, we must love selfishly because only by knowing ourselves and our own necessities can we recognize another's and love them.

That inward journey of self-discovery must be taken by each individual in the course of a lifetime and, on a vast scale, by the whole of our species. Just as the tiny jellied blob of a foetus in the womb roughly encapsulates something of all life's development from microscopic protozoa through fishy gills and reptile brain into a recognizably modern infant homo sapiens, so each human being from infancy on rehearses humanity's physical and mental progress: the triumphant change from crawling on all fours to standing on two legs and the slow psychic advance from an inability to distinguish between self and others to the awesome realization of total separateness. That inward journey, like a vast inverted pyramid, began with its wide base encompassing the dawn of tribal Australopithecus and narrows through the ages until it peaks at our own time, the age of individualism, when separateness has become a playwright's cliché, artists paint the inside of their own heads, shrinks are kings of the castle and some of us spend our entire lives scrabbling about inside ourselves for revelations of our human potential. But on the horizon, like a huge spaceship settling towards earth, there is another pyramid whose wide base spreads dimly into the future. We have come inwards and now, perhaps, our children and our great-grandchildren can start the voyage out again, trying to reach again, with all the hard-earned knowledge acquired upon the way, something of the same state of mind that our earliest ancestors possessed through the simpler demands of survival. We have reached the zenith of inwardness and see its first rotting edges – narcissism, loneliness, greed, sterility. It is time to begin the outward trek again, away from the prison of self to the freedom of other people. Survival demands it – there is already too great an inner gulf between each one of us and our peers and that threatens dangers that many eventually wreck our planet and our species.

Charles Darwin, the first man to chart our inward journey from tribal ape to isolated modern man, also glimpsed the eventual need to retrace our footprints:

If man progresses to culture and smaller tribes are unified into larger societies, then the simplest consideration on the part of every individual will tell him that he must extend his social instincts and sympathies to all members of the same nation, even if they are unknown to him personally. Once this point is reached there is only an artificial barrier preventing him from extending his sympathies to all people of all nations and all races.

And Arnold Gehlen added, 'The ethos of altruism is the family one; it first exists within the extended family but it is capable of extension until the idea embraces the whole of humanity.' Freud believed that war could be averted by activating 'all those forces which establish emotional bonds' and the anthropologist Eibl-Eibesfeldt, talking of the future, comments, 'Many deeply rooted impulses may become obsolete, having lost their species-preserving function. Aggression towards the "outsider" may be one such.'

My own belief is that the growing equality of women and our participation in human affairs may add weight and direction to the outward journey. There is much more of a tribal consciousness in us than in men, we are the ones who like to do things with other people, who prefer co-operation to dominance, who gain pleasure from the approval rather than the competitiveness of others, who struggle in our increasing equality to avoid the hierarchical male structures. According to surveys, we even need less personal space around us than men, we relish physical contact, we do not keep our distance. We are, in other words, well-fitted to encourage that journey back to some form of shared living and feeling, once we have equipped ourselves with an ego that need not be egoistic and moved from the ghetto of emotion into our heritage of reason.

As it is, all of us are lonely and bewildered. Our constant and often unwanted companions upon our inward journey have been the discoveries that underline mankind's diminishing importance as a species. Once upon a time any human being, however humble his status among his own kind, could regard himself as one among the kings of the earth and rulers of the universe. Then came Copernicus and Galileo to tell us that our planet was not the centre of that universe but one among other planets and a mere encircling courtier to the sun. As we reeled from this cosmic shock, Darwin appeared and reluctantly informed us that we were not only no great shakes in space but that we were not made on the sixth day by God, modelled upon his ineffable self. We were, in fact, descendants of animals, born of apes, related to marmosets, our beginnings not hallowed in the skies above but forged in the seas, among the blind jellies. Ever more humbling discoveries followed thick and fast so that, today, we are twice cursed – we feel the terrible burden of our individual consciousness at the same time as we know that our span of life weighs no more in real terms than a mayfly's day.

And, curious paradox, at just the time when many men have more control over their personal, social and political lives than ever before, when even reproduction can be ordered, when all the resources of the State we have created can be directed towards physical survival into older and older age, when even disease, even death itself, could have an end, only now are we forced to speculate that all this apparent autonomy may signify nothing. It is as if a hedgehog mutated into the most self-conscious of all hedgehogs, aware like no other hedgehog before him of his quintessential hedgehoggedness and realized at last that he was, after all, only a hedgehog. Despair.

But out of that despair, out of that anguished self-consciousness, came for the first time the spores of real love. Many ingredients for its proper growth and eventual flowering are still absent but something down there in the dark earth stirs. At least some of us are no longer too poor to love – one of love's main prerequisites is a life of reasonable comfort. We, the ordinary people, have been handed a myriad pretty definitions of love by theologians, artists, philosophers and others of the fortunate, all of them powerful or privileged or extraordinary, almost all of them men – and reading between their lines it is easy to see that each one of them assumes love is a mightily exclusive club not to be joined by coarse-grained peasants, an emotion whose natural habitat is the silk-hung houses of the rich.

These men were right about us but wrong about themselves. If love was unknown to the masses, it was equally unknown to the rich. Games they had, the thrills and spills of seduction they had, sacrifice and worship they had, masochism and sadism, lust and Weltschmertz, poetry and passion were theirs. But true love was as absent from the château and the Schloss as it was from the barnyards of the poor. Passion, that extreme emotion considered in our society as the highest manifestation of love as we like it, uncontrollable, irrational, a true religious possession, may have to do with narcissism or the death wish but it has nothing to do with the love necessary for our future good. Apart from its general uselessness, it contains a high proportion of hatred and gives those in its grip very little happiness. I quote two women who have suffered from it:

On the night of the storm – oh it was terrible, you have no idea, the waves lashing over the front, the wind crashing the water about, a noise that would deafen you – David was drunk as always and started saying he was going out there, going to see what it was like. He pushed open the front door and disappeared up the street, which was already running with water. I didn't stop him, I didn't say a word. I thought to myself, good, perhaps he will drown and that will solve my problem. I can tell the children he died being brave and I will be free at last. I often dream that he has died. I couldn't bear him to leave me for someone else but I would be quite relieved if he died.

And another woman, who murdered her woman lover:

I stood outside her door, ringing the bell, holding my knife. When she came out, I stabbed her and that very moment, as the knife was going in, my love for her just stopped. I felt nothing at all as she fell. I couldn't think why I was there at all.

The woman lived for another ten days, her murderess was taken to see her in hospital before she died, knowing she was dying. What did she feel? 'Absolutely nothing. Nothing.'

Obviously, in many ways, passion is the opposite of love. Its paroxysms of jealousy and possessiveness can cause such pain that, like an alien and lethal growth, the sufferer attempts to cut it out, either in fantasies of death or actual murder. And many of us, far less enthralled than these two women, share something of their feelings when passion grips us, overwhelming our selves. In some ways our wish to escape, our fantasies of death to the beloved (however quickly suppressed), are healthy and understandable. We are fighting to retain some independence against an emotion that threatens our whole individual being.

Romantic love, though gentler, takes no more heed of the beloved. It is not a song of praise and adoration for another but a paean to the self that is too rare, too sensitive, ever to bestow its heart upon anyone but a being equally rare. Romance contains a large proportion of sublimated sex but sex is too basic, too much a reminder of our animal heritage to be admitted by so sensitive a soul. The Christian Church, with its diatribes against sex, prepared the ground for the romantic excrescence by forcing an honest drive underground.

The relationships we must learn to make on our return journey to a new sort of tribalism must have as their source a different and more flexible heterosexual or homosexual love, with its roots in equality and reason. To start with, this new love will be unconnected with reproduction, since most people will at most only reproduce themselves and some will not reproduce at all. As Dr Robert Morison of Cornell University has said, 'Once sex and reproduction are separated, society will have to struggle with defining the nature of interpersonal relationships which have no long-term social point', and to that we must add the future prospect of living well over the century – gerontologists are already predicting not only an average life-span of 125 years but the eventual possibility of averting death itself except in the case of lethal accidents. Yet if extreme adaptability involving the minimum innate behaviour and the maximum learning has already been the key to our prolific survival, presumably our sexual roles are equally flexible, given the chance. Human history, based on human communication and increased co-operation, is not so much a biological as a cultural evolution and since there is every reason to think that gender, sexual roles and therefore social roles are culturally induced, there is every reason to believe they can change, particularly since the future of our evolution may well rest in knowing more, using the neo-cortex to accumulate more knowledge and to deepen its effectiveness in general.

Somehow, in the future, we have to solve a paradox by uniting two former opposites. The brain itself gives us a clue and most futurologists of whatever discipline agree that neuro-physiology is the science of the future. There is astonishingly little difference, chemically, anatomically and physiologically, between the brains of the three and a half million human beings on this planet, whether they are geniuses or mentally retarded, yet the differences in performance and behaviour between human beings demonstrate what Steven Rose called 'the essential unity of humans and their essential individuality', stemming from some still-mysterious region of the apparently similar brains.

So we already have all the necessary physical, genetic and cerebral equipment to manage the paradox, which is to fit together what have so far been mutually exclusive states: the tribal psyche that gains its identity and satisfaction by merging with others and the highly-developed individual ego of the twentieth century, isolated, introverted and uniquely self-conscious. Neither is desirable alone but together they may shape a better future.

In evolutionary terms, an emotion of goodwill towards others has always been a necessary tool of survival. United we stand, divided we fall. Any emotion, any act that militates for peaceful co-operation, whether in the drudgery of the worker ant or the mutual grooming of the great apes is selected by an indifferent Nature simply because those animals who best practise it fulfil any species's first imperative – to survive, to reproduce. Socio-biologists reduce all signs of altruistic behaviour to a single formula: the individual is the gene's way of producing other genes, in other words our instinctual task in life is to pass on our genes and then cherish them as best we can, whether in our own children or our closest relatives or our tribe. But whatever reason or method we back, one fact is clear. Never in our whole history has mankind so badly needed that highest form of co-operation called love. My generation, the one born under the sign of the nuclear mushroom, has been the first to realize and live with the knowledge that hatred, fear and aggression between men no longer merely threatens an individual, a tribe, even a nation. Now and in the future these destructive emotions herald the elimination of our whole planet. And even if, in an access of optimism, we put aside the nuclear threat, we are merely left with equally inevitable, though less immediate, threats. Pollution, the destruction of our seas and rivers, the piercing of the ozone barrier that keeps us all from burning up, the decimation of those other species with whom we share our planet and on whom we depend far more than we now recognize for survival, the rape of the earth's riches which give us anything from warmth and health to clothes and transport, and the ever-present possibility that some act of ours, scientific or purely emotional, will create havoc in the very genes of our species.

The embryonic form of love which was actually an attempt at mutual co-operation has been around a long time in man's history, inherited from the apes and refined by language. Each individual was motivated to survive, discovered that his chances were enhanced if others were around to help, scratched their backs so that they might scratch his and called the resulting emotions – gratitude, the appeasement of a lonely helplessness – love, when it was merely an affection, a mutual fellow-feeling. Or rather, the fortunate upon the earth called it love. The others, the majority, living at subsistence levels, just got on with things and gave them no labels. Love was always dependent upon some leisure and a full stomach and so it is today. Even so, a question arises. If co-operation and a mild affection plus the bonding of sex was enough and more than enough to enable our species to become lords of the planet, why should we ever bother with more? Why even mention love, never mind carry on about how love itself must evolve to a higher emotion altogether? Who needs it, false or true?

It seems to me that the facts of the matter are these. Romantic and passionate love evolved from the affection bred by co-operation as co-operation itself began to wither. In an industrial society dedicated to private and not public enterprise, man is pitted against man rather than with him. As individualism and isolation grew, individual love between one and one became the booby prize, the domestic consolation in an outside world that asked the individual only for his labour and rewarded him only with things. As human beings became cogs in society's machine, the need to reaffirm some special identity, to retain some small autonomy, translated itself into the love we know today, the heady mixture that gives us a reason for living and acts on our nervous systems in the same way as sniffing isobutyl nitrate, the poor man's cocaine – lightheadedness and a sudden rush that makes the heart race and the body quiver. Love as the popper of the people. Its chemical ingredients are largely sex with a hefty dash of egoism, boredom and an eye to the main chance. Like the drug itself, the effects are intense and brief.

But it is already becoming obvious that the old sort of love no longer fits in with our changing needs, whether those needs are particular and personal or general, as an evolutionary tool. Above all, it does not fit in with the change in women. One of the strongest drives behind the women's movement is more inward than a wish for equal legislation, opportunities, education and wages, though all these form a part. What women want above all is to become real, to discard the mannered feminine mask and reveal the human being beneath, a person who is neither a Virgin Mary to be put on a pedestal nor a Lilith to be fearfully desired nor a Martha to wait at table, but simply a person sufficient unto herself, with her own talents and inadequacies, her own idiosyncrasies, good, bad or indifferent.

And the current recipe for love, whether romantic or passionate, in no way answers this need; indeed, the twain shall never meet. In this form of love, there is only at most room for one real person (though the headiest experience of it is when neither is real) and by custom and convention, plus the fact that the woman is still regarded as unreal because unequal by outside institutions, that real person is usually the man. In order to be loved today, a woman must forfeit what small reality she has managed to dig up for herself.

Increasingly, as the material benefits of the fight for equality make themselves felt, giving women financial independence, better education, more chance to fulfil career ambitions and more control over reproduction, women are rejecting the false role romantic love demands of them, as they can more and more afford to reject what romantic love gave them – security at a price and a brief filling of the ego vacuum. Often, neither partner benefited. It is not a lot of fun to awake from a dream of fair things and find mortgage payments in the letter box and kids wailing upstairs and a stranger lying on the pillow next to yours, but a stranger sans excitement.

Rumours reach us that because women are demanding something more substantial of love than hearts and flowers, nipping the pretty mirage in the bud, men are becoming impotent, homosexual or otherwise turned off. All very sad but entirely predictable. Any change in social patterns disturbs the generation involved, where it be for good or bad. Marilyn French's heroine Mira, in *The Women's Room*, ends up after her struggle for identity learning to accept loneliness as a better alternative than the poison apple of love, and so it is. Kingsley Amis's hero Jake, in *Jake's Thing*, can't be bothered to continue the strenuous cure for impotency prescribed by his tame sexologist because he decides he does't like women anyway, or not the new, pushy women he imagines around him. In other words Mira, in being true to herself, can no longer arouse either sexual desire or love in men like Jake who need the carefully false feminine archetype, unchallenging and submissive, before they can want or get an erection.

The inequality, the falsities and the separation between men and women are disappearing, albeit slowly, and with them the sexual signals men are conditioned to expect. Conditioning, however powerful, dies with the conditioned individual and a new generation will not need to centre its feelings upon old tricks, however prettily done up in buttons or bows and the equivalent trappings of masculinity.

The interesting thing is that the slow emergence of true love does not predicate some higher version of morality. No sudden conversions, no lights upon the road to Damascus are in any way necessary. A new generation with new standards of loving will not come about as a result of some mystical mutation or spiritual growth, though these may well follow. The facts are more practical. As equality becomes commonplace between men and women, they themselves will perforce change from stereotypes, however successful or unsuccessful, into ordinary human beings, each one rather different from the next. Standard sexual roles – the breadwinner, the housewife and mother – already blurred, will eventually disappear and with them will go the suppression or exaggeration of parts of the individual character made necessary by those roles. And as these masks, stylized as the masks of Japanese Kabuki, slip to reveal the human face behind, romantic love, so heavily dependent upon an artificial façade and predictable masculine or feminine behaviour, will die from starvation. Already it is showing the first signs of incipient malnutrition. When, added to that, children are raised in equality and mothers, secure in their own identity, no longer pass their fears and inferiorities on to their daughters or too great an admiration on to their sons; when both parents are equally concerned with the upbringing of children and therefore ensure that those children cannot divide their own emotions between the sexes and discard one whole area, we will have bred a race of human beings differentiated by their own personalities rather than their genitalia. The old war-cry of sexists – *vive la différence* – actually implied exactly the opposite; the rigid division of an infinite variety of people into just two categories, male and female. *Vive la similarité.* Variety will replace conformity and variety, apart from being an evolutionary must, forces each potential lover to take stock of an individual rather than searching for the stereotyped ideal of a whole sex.

Nor is this change dependent solely on a conscious wish for change. Evolution has always had a voracious appetite for variety, it is literally the spice of life, offering as it does a wide menu for natural selection. And it is becoming clear to many of us that the old stereotypes of male and female are increasingly a positive threat to the well-being of the race and the earth. Women, confined to a domestic and biological cage, produce unwanted children to crowd an already over-populated world, while their own abilities wither on the hearth. Men, driven by out-dated standards of virility, continue to denude the planet and threaten each other with uncontemplatable war. Love between such men and such women serves only their own artificial needs and seals them off in their *folie à deux* from the rest of the world instead of involving them more deeply, as real love would do. Our planetary problems are rapidly becoming too serious to permit the net-curtain mentality of the average self-satisfied couple as they peep out at trouble and hastily withdraw, safe in the certainty that God himself blesses their cosy twosome and demands nothing more than its continuation, properly seeded with kiddies.

That is not to say that monogamy is on its way out, only that monogamy as we know it today – sacrosanct, het-erosexual, reproductive, lifelong and almost always a retreat from life – no longer adequately fulfils either the individuals concerned or society. All research done recently, whether anthropological, paediatric, psychiatric, criminal or social, arrives at the same conclusion: human beings develop most fully and happily if they can feel loved as children by one or two constantly present adults and, as adults themselves, re-produce the same closeness with one other adult. But there is nothing to prove that years of monogamy with the *same* adult are necessarily beneficial. Lifelong monogamy may be nice for the Church and useful for the tax-collector but it has many drawbacks for the individual, who is a learning as well as an imprinted being. As we change and learn, from youth to old age, we must give ourselves room for that change. Like snakes, we need occasionally to shed our old skins and often we cannot do that if we are tied by bonds of guilt to an outgrown love. None of us grows at the same speed or in the same way and the chances of a parallel development with one other human being are not great. But nor does this imply a lack of love or some pervasive shame. Each of us may give another person love and help in inner growth for a while. But in a changing world, with changing people, why should we expect that love to last for ever or denigrate it if it does not? Why should love, once a mansion, be made into a cage through false expectations of what love is?

Lifelong monogamy has other drawbacks, even when it works, perhaps *especially* when it works. In a cold and problematic world it is all too easy to withdraw into the cosiness of a familiar love, leaving those problems for others to solve. We have a genetic need for other people; monogamous love, in attempting to assuage that need with one other person, may not only sour into neuroses or a mutual flattery that reduces both partners, making them fear the outside world, but may also isolate us from our fellows and allow us to care less about their fate. When my husband is away from home, I turn in need to my friends, even to strangers. I become vulnerable once again to their larger opinion of me. I see myself as others, more coldly, see me. On his return my instinct is to warm myself at his me-centred love, to soothe my slightly bruised ego. Luckily for me, he does not need to build me up for his own ego and so he is not all *that* warm, just warm enough. He leaves place in me for others, because he himself has place for others.

All this – changing women, the danger of stereotypes and intractable monogamy, the needs of our race and our planet in the future – implies one imperative. We must leave adolescence behind and grow up. It is absolutely vital, if we are to continue to exist in some comfort upon our earth, that we take a giant step into true adulthood, learn to filter the emotions through our reasoning capacities and learn that survival itself rests on knowing who we are, respecting others' space and endeavouring justly to balance our own and others' needs.

And this is where love truly comes into its own as an evolutionary tool. Parental love teaches children one vital fact: that they are loved and lovable and therefore can themselves love. But the love between adults differs in one absolute from parental love: it is conditional, or should be. We find out who we are by feeling our outlines against other people, by finding out who we are not. In loving but honest eyes we see prisms of our own vague face, slowly we put the prisms together and distinguish certain unchanging features, form certain principles. Inside, a centre begins to form and once it is firmly established, roots well grown, blossoms flourishing, we can turn from it towards others with a real sense of where we differ and where we are the same. And once we know that, once we respect ourselves, it becomes impossible to accept another who violates our beliefs and ourselves. A weak ego, a weak hold on reality, opens the doors to any passing stranger who flatters us enough and makes us feel real. A strong ego, a firm knowledge of who we are, demands conditions of that stranger, demands a similarity of belief and behaviour and can discard what it does not respect, even at the price of rejecting easy flattery.

And that is what true love is there to help us do. Properly informed, lovingly detached, centred respectfully in itself, it provides us with a real reflection of ourselves, to help us grow. Principles do not need to be suppressed for fear of displeasing, for fear of loss, because when the crunch comes, we can cope alone.

Love cannot thrive in inequality or extreme poverty. It requires enough leisure for introspection and enough introspection for empathy. It demands that the individual feels a certain control over his life because, in too great a storm, we tend to seek any refuge. It thrives on honesty and therefore must do away with great need, since need drives out honesty. It is rational, it knows its own roots, it is moral and controllable because it stems from the head and not the heart. Any resemblance it bears to love as we know it today is purely fictional.

And true love is still in embryo, fragile compared to other ties because it derives no strength from more ancient needs. Its roots are not in the past but in the future. It is a beginning, a new survival mechanism slowly evolving to suit new circumstances.

Select Bibliography

When writing a book of opinion, it is impossible to tell which authors were of most help in the initial research – those who are straightforwardly informative, those whose ideas inspire or those who most irritate and provoke. In addition to those listed, I am of course grateful to many other writers whose thoughts I absorbed long before this book was planned.

AMIS, KINGSLEY. *Jake's Thing*, Hutchinson, 1978.

ARDREY, ROBERT. *The Territorial Imperative*, Collins, 1967/Fontana, 1969.

——*African Genesis*, Collins, 1961/Fontana, 1969.

ARMS, SUZANNE. *Immaculate Deception*, San Francisco Books/Houghton Mifflin, 1975.

ATKINS, SUSAN. *Child of Satan, Child of God*, Hodder & Stoughton, 1978.

BENEDICT, RUTH. *Patterns of Culture*, Routledge, 1935.

CAUDWELL, CHRISTOPER. *Studies and Further Studies in a Dying Culture*, Monthly Review Press, 1971.

COMER, LEE. *Wedlocked Women*, Feminist Books, 1974.

COX, SUE. *Female Psychology: The Emerging Self*, Science Research Associates, 1976.

DAY, BETH. *Sexual Life Between Blacks and Whites*, Collins, 1974.

DINNERSTEIN, DOROTHY. *The Rocking of the Cradle and the Ruling of the World*, Souvenir Press, 1978.

EIBL-EIBESFELDT, IRENAUS. *Love and Hate*, Methuen, 1972.

EPTON, NINA. *Love and the French*, Cassell, 1959.

—— *Love and the English*, Cassell, 1960.

FRENCH, MARILYN. *The Women's Room*, André Deutsch, 1978.

FREUD, SIGMUND. *Sexuality and the Psychology of Love*, Collier Books, New York, 1963.

GISSING, GEORGE. *New Grub Street*, Smith Elder, 1891/Penguin English Library, 1968.

HARRISON, G. A., WEINER, J. S., TANNER, J. M. and BARNICOT, N. A., eds. *Human Biology*, Oxford University Press, 1977.

HEER, FRIEDRICH. *The Mediaeval World*, Cardinal, 1974.

JONAS, DORIS and JONAS, DAVID. *Sex and Status*, Hodder & Stoughton, 1976.

KOESTLER, ARTHUR. *Janus*, Huchinson, 1978.

LEE, PATRICK and STEWART, ROBERT SUSSMAN, eds. *Sex Differences*, Urizen Books, New York, 1977.

LÉVI-STRAUSS, CLAUDE. *The Elementary Structures of Kinship*, Eyre & Spottiswoode, 1969.

MAQUET, JACQUES J. P. *The Premise of Inequality in Ruanda*, Oxford University Press, 1961.

MAYOR, F. M. *The Rector's Daughter*, Hogarth Press, 1924.

MILLER, JEAN BAKER. *Towards a New Psychology of Women*, Beacon Press, Boston, Mass., 1976.

MILLETT, KATE. *Sita*, Virago, 1977.

MOFFAT, MARY JANE and PAINTER, CHARLOTTE, eds. *Revelations – Diaries of Women*, Vintage Books, New York, 1975.

MORGAN, ELAINE. *The Descent of Woman*, Souvenir Press, 1972/Corgi, 1974.

NAPIER, PRUE. *Monkeys and Apes*, Hamlyn, 1970.

O'FAOLAIN, JULIA and MARTINES, LAURO, eds. *Not in God's Image*, Temple Smith, 1973.

PARLEE, MARY BROWN. 'Social Factors in the Psychology of Menstruation, Birth and Menopause', *Primary Care*, Vol. 3, Part 3, pp. 477–90, 1976.

PEARSALL, RONALD. *The Worm in the Bud*, Weidenfeld & Nicolson, 1969/Penguin, 1971.

PEELE, STANTON and BRODSKY, ARCHIE. *Love and Addiction*, Abacus, 1977.

POWER, EILEEN. *Mediaeval Women*, Cambridge University Press, 1975.

PREVIN, DORY. *Midnight Baby*, Elm Tree Books, 1977.

REED, EVELYN. *Woman's Evolution*, Pathfinder Press, 1975.

ROSE, STEVEN. *The Conscious Brain*, Weidenfeld & Nicolson, 1973/Penguin, 1976.

DE ROUGEMENT, DENIS. *Passion and Society,* Faber & Faber, 1940.

SAGAN, CARL. *The Dragons of Eden,* Hodder & Stoughton, 1978.

SARGANT, WILLIAM. *Battle for the Mind,* Heinemann, 1957.

—— *The Mind Possessed,* Heinemann, 1973.

SCHAPERA, ISAAC. *Married Life in an African Tribe,* Faber & Faber, 1940/Penguin, 1971.

SCHEFLIN, A. and OPTON, E., JR. *The Mind Manipulators,* Paddington Press, 1978.

SERENY, GITTA. *Into That Darkness: From Mercy Killing to Mass Murder,* André Deutsch, 1974/Pan, 1977.

SHORTER, EDWARD. *The Making of the Modern Family,* Collins, 1976/Fontana, 1977.

SHUTTLE, PENELOPE and REDGROVE, PETER. *The Wise Wound,* Gollancz, 1978.

SKINNER, B. F. *About Behaviourism,* Cape, 1975.

SUTTIE, IAN. *Origins of Love and Hate,* Kegan Paul, 1935.

TURNBULL, COLIN. *The Mountain People,* Cape, 1973.

WEINSTEIN, FRED and PLATT, GERALD. *The Wish to be Free,* University of California Press, 1973.

WILSON, PATRICK. *Murderess,* Michael Joseph, 1971.

Index

217